THEOPOLITICAL IMAGINATION

THEOPOLITICAL
IMAGINATION

William T. Cavanaugh

B L O O M S B U R Y
LONDON • NEW DELHI • NEW YORK • SYDNEY

Bloomsbury T&T Clark
An imprint of Bloomsbury Publishing Plc

50 Bedford Square	1385 Broadway
London	New York
WC1B 3DP	NY 10018
UK	USA

www.bloomsbury.com

First published 2002
Reprinted 2004, 2005, 2007, 2008 (twice), 2010, 2011
Reprinted by Bloomsbury Academic 2013

© T & T Clark, 2002

British Library Cataloguing-in-Publication Data
A catalogue record for this book is available from the British Library.

ISBN: HB: 978-0-567-08877-2
PB: 978-0-567-08897-0

Library of Congress Cataloging-in-Publication Data
A catalog record for this book is available from the Library of Congress.

Typeset by BookEns Ltd, Royston Herts
Printed and bound in Great Britain

For Finnian and Declan

CONTENTS

PREFACE AND ACKNOWLEDGEMENTS

The idea for this book began when a Swiss publisher asked me to gather some of my essays for translation into French. I took the suggestion as an opportunity to re-form some related essays that have received some attention into a continuous argument about the shape of the Christian political imagination today. The material of the original essays has been rearranged and, in places, rewritten to fit this purpose. I am happy that this material is now available in the more accessible form of a book. The book is brief, however, and may be seen as a promissory note toward treating these themes in more depth in the future.

I would like to thank Gregory Solari of Editions Ad Solem in Geneva for first proposing the idea for this book. It is available from Ad Solem, in slightly different form, under the title *Eucharistie et mondialisation: La liturgie comme acte politique*. I would also like to thank Stratford Caldecott of T. & T. Clark for shepherding the English version into print. Various people made insightful comments on earlier drafts; I am indebted to Frederick Bauerschmidt, Michael Baxter, Daniel Bell, John Berkman, James Fodor, Stanley Hauerwas, Michael Hollerich, Reinhard Hütter, D. Stephen Long, Gerald Schlabach, and Paul Wojda for helping me think through these issues. As always, my wife Tracy has been my unfailing support. This book is dedicated to our children, Finnian and Declan, who for us have brought the reality of living in communion home.

INTRODUCTION
DISCIPLINED IMAGINATIONS OF SPACE
AND TIME

Politics is a practice of the imagination. Sometimes politics is the 'art of the possible,' but it is always an art, and engages the imagination just as art does. We are often fooled by the seeming solidity of the materials of politics, its armies and offices, into forgetting that these materials are marshalled by acts of the imagination. How does a provincial farm boy become persuaded that he must travel as a soldier to another part of the world and kill people he knows nothing about? He must be convinced of the reality of borders, and imagine himself deeply, mystically, united to a wider national community that stops abruptly at those borders. The nation-state is, as Benedict Anderson has shown, one important and historically contingent type of 'imagined community' around which our conceptions of politics tend to gather.[1]

This little book is an exercise in a different kind of political imagination, one that is rooted in the Christian story. In three chapters I will analyse the state, civil society, and globalization, respectively. I will not treat these themes as givens with their own proper autonomy with which the Church must simply deal. I will instead display the state, civil society, and globalization as three disciplined and interrelated ways of

---

[1] Benedict Anderson, *Imagined Communities: Reflections on the Origin and Spread of Nationalism* (London: Verso, 1991).

1

imagining space and time. Far from merely 'secular' insti-tutions and processes, these ways of imagining organize bodies around stories of human nature and human destiny which have deep theological analogues. In other words, sup-posedly 'secular' political theory is really theology in disguise. As I will show in Chapter 1, for example, the modern state is built upon a soteriology of rescue from violence. To see this as a false or 'heretical' soteriology then opens the doors to a reimagination of space and time along true theological lines.

As has been pointed out by Philip Abrams and others,[2] the state as such does not exist. What exists are buildings and aeroplanes and tax forms and border patrols. What mobilizes these into a project called 'nation-state' is a disciplined imagination of a community occupying a particular space with a common conception of time, a common history and a common destiny of salvation from peril. This imagination is not a mere symbol of something more real, an immaterial 'superstructure' which reflects a material 'base.' There is no way to separate material and cultural production. The political imagination is simply the condition of possibility for the organization of bodies in a society.

Modern politics was not simply discovered by making a proper separation of the sacred and the secular which had become improperly confused, as one would separate the element iron from its ore. Modern politics was not discovered but imagined, invented. As I will show in the first chapter, what we call 'religion,' a fundamentally interior disposition of the individual toward the transcendent, was also an invention of fairly recent origin. To identify politics and religion as acts

---

[2] Philip Abrams, 'Notes on the Difficulty of Studying the State,' *Journal of Historical Sociology* 1, no. 1 (March 1988), p. 77; also Ralph Miliband, *The State in Capitalist Society: An Analysis of the Western System of Power* (New York: Basic Books, 1969).

of the imagination is to recognize their historical contingency, and thus give hope that things do not necessarily have to be the way they are. It is also to put the political and the theological imaginations on an equal footing, as it were, and thus open an opportunity for the theological imagination to enact alternative space-times.

Too often the modern Christian theological imagination has got lost in the stories that sustain modern politics. The Christendom model assumed the legitimacy of the nation-state and tried to preserve the established position of the Church in guiding it. The New Christendom model assumed the legitimacy of the autonomy of the temporal, and tried to influence the political order through the Christian as an indi-vidual. 'Political theology' and 'public theology' have assumed the legitimacy of the separation of the state from civil society, and tried to situate the Church as one more interest group within civil society. None of these models has fundamentally called into question the theological legitimacy of the imagination of modern politics.

The reality of globalization may finally be providing us with an opportunity to recast our imagination of space and time. Transnational commerce and information promise/ threaten to create one global village. The borders which once seemed so solidly to define the territorial nation-state – borders which marked out a 'public square' for political debate, borders which sharply divided domestic policy from foreign policy and fellow-citizens from strangers – these borders have now begun to appear quite porous. Sovereignty is becoming best understood 'less as a territorially defined barrier than a bargaining resource for a politics characterized by complex transnational networks.'[3] This does not mean the

---

[3] R. O. Keohane, quoted in David Held, Anthony McGrew, David Goldblatt and Jonathan Perraton, *Global Transformations: Politics, Economics, and Culture* (Stanford, CA: Stanford University Press, 1999), p. 9.

simple demise of the nation-state; as I will argue in Chapter 3, globalization in fact marks the hyperextension of some of the most dangerous pathologies of the nation-state. Nevertheless, globalization is in some respects a rupture with the dominant mode of seeing the political. The fluidity of the current situation at least offers Christians an opportunity to rethink the dominant modes of Christian engagement with the political.

I am increasingly convinced that for Christians the only fruitful way of moving forward in this context is to tap the theological resources of the Christian tradition for more radical imaginings of space and time. No longer can we accept the positioning of Christian theology by secular political theologies in the name of a false and murderous civic peace. Christian theology must renounce all implication in the means of violence, but simultaneously – *and for the same reason* – theology cannot surrender its claim to be simply about the way the world is, which includes what we have learned to call the political and the social. Once the imaginations underlying modern political processes have been exposed as false theologies, we can begin to recover true theological imaginings of space and time around which to enact communities of solidarity and resistance.

In the chapters that follow, I will suggest a focus on the Eucharist as one privileged site for the Christian spatio-temporal imagination. With regard to space, a body is enacted in the Eucharistic celebration, a body that – as liturgical – is public. Precisely as a *body*, the body of Christ is not confinable to a spiritual 'meaning' secreted away in the soul of the individual believer. In the Eucharist people are gathered into a community in which the calculus of individual and group is overcome by a mutual participation. Furthermore, Eucharistic communities worldwide form one *Catholica* which, though universal, is always and only enacted at the local level. The global and the local are refracted in such a way that one becomes more united to the universal the more one is tied to the life of a particular local community. With regard to time, the Eucharist is both an act of 'dangerous memory' of the past death of Jesus Christ at the hands of the powers and of his resurrection, as well as the eschatological anticipation of the future Kingdom of God. This 'memory of the future,' in John Zizioulas' phrase, interrupts the uniform march of time on which both capitalism and the nation-state depend, a time that is end-less, that is, without termination or telos. At the Eucharist we are fellow-citizens not merely of other currently living Americans or Germans or Britons but of those in heaven who have gone before us and toward whom we now strain forward (Phil. 3.13). In this eschatological view we must regard all human beings, Christians and non-Christians alike, as at least potential members of the body of Christ. The way the Eucharist thus structures space and time has radical implications for the way we imagine the political, implica-tions which I spell out briefly in the following chapters.

Recent Christian attempts to overcome the privatization of Christianity have largely failed for a number of interrelated reasons. The most significant such reason is their inability to break decisively with the Enlightenment story of seculariza-tion. This story assumes that directly politicized theology is inherently dangerous and violent, and that the modern era has done a tremendous service for peace in separating power from religion. The task of my first chapter is to show that this story is historically and theologically false. The myth of early modern 'religious wars' from which the modern state has saved us is historically untrue. The rise of the modern secular state is a historically contingent event that has produced more, not less, violence. It has done so not by secularizing politics, but by supplanting the imagination of the body of Christ with a heretical theology of salvation through the state.

Many attempts at salvaging the 'public' nature of Christianity proceed by carving out a space for the church in civil society, a supposed sphere of free participation that stands independent of the state. Nevertheless, Christian discourse cannot be directly inserted into the public debate. As I will argue in my second chapter, however, the overlap between state power and civil society increasingly renders the distinction of state and civil society problematic as a form of empirical political description. Furthermore, the imagination of such a sphere of free participation polices and distorts the gospel by translating the radical demands of discipleship into 'public reason' which is not valid if it contradicts the ends of the nation-state. The exclusion of Christian theological discourse from the putative public forum is done in the name of a 'secular' neutrality which in fact marginalizes the body of Christ in favour of an imagined community, a false public body, centred in the state.

In Chapter 3 I take the discussion beyond the nation-state and address globalization, which has only recently entered into Christian theological discourse. There are some who have hailed globalization as a new catholicity which moves us beyond the nation-state-centred pathologies of modern politics. There is an apparent universality aborning in the rapidly globalizing world which would overcome the particularism of a political discourse bounded by national sovereignty. I argue, however, that globalization is in fact not the end of the nation-state but the hyperextension of the nation-state project of the dominance of the universal over the particular, that is, the subsumption of local communal spaces under the authority of the sovereign territorial state. Globalization is a false catholicity that tries to smooth over the complex refraction of local and universal in the Christian conception of a truly catholic body.

The overall argument of this book is in no way an attempt

to exonerate the historical church for its many sins. It calls instead for a set of practices which entail a way of repentance for Christian complicity with violence. Expressly theological politics is of course not immune to violence; it all depends on what kind of theology and what kind of politics is being imagined. Negatively, I want only to argue that the separation of power from any transcendent moorings has not made the world less violent, but has only made the violence more arbitrary and more intense. In exposing some of the false theological imaginings of modern politics, I hope to give hope to the reader that the iron cage of modernity does not inevitably hold us in its grip. I focus on the Eucharist as an alternative imagining of space and time which builds up a body of resistance to violence, the body of Christ. This is a body that is wounded, broken by the powers and princi- palities and poured out in blood offering upon this stricken earth. But this is also a body crossed by the resurrection, a sign of the startling irruption of the Kingdom into historical time and the disruptive presence of Christ the King to the politics of the world.

1

THE MYTH OF THE STATE AS SAVIOUR

Humankind was created for communion, but is everywhere divided. For the purposes of this chapter, this opening statement will serve as a somewhat bold summary of the book of Genesis, chapters 1–11. The reader will recognize an intentional parallel with one of the most famous opening lines of modern intellectual history, that of Rousseau's *The Social Contract*: 'Man was born free, but is everywhere in bondage.'[1] Although at first sight Genesis and *The Social Contract* seem to be about quite different tasks, both are similarly engaged with foundational stories of human cooperation and division. Modernity is unaccustomed to regarding political theory as mythological in character. The modern state is, however, founded on certain stories of nature and human nature, the origins of human conflict, and the remedies for such conflict in the enactment of the state itself. In this chapter I will read these stories against the Christian stories of creation, fall, and redemption, and argue that both ultimately have the same goal: salvation of humankind from the divisions that plague us. The modern state is best understood, I will attempt to show, as an alternative soteriology to that of the Church. Both soteriologies pursue peace and an end to division by the enactment of a social body; the foundation of the state is based on a widely-accepted myth about the necessity of the

---

[1] Jean Jacques Rousseau, *The Social Contract*, trans. Willmoore Kendall (South Bend, IN: Gateway Editions, 1954), p. 2 [Bk I, ch. 1].

state to save Europe from the 'Wars of Religion' in the sixteenth and seventeenth centuries. Nevertheless I will argue in this chapter that the usual way these wars are narrated is false, and that the state body is a simulacrum, a false copy, of the Body of Christ.

By 'state' I mean to denote that peculiar institution which has arisen in the last four centuries in which a centralized and abstract power holds a monopoly over physical coercion within a geographically defined territory. I am aware of the danger in ignoring the differences between actual states, or between states in theory and states in practice. Nevertheless, I think it is a useful exercise to consider in general terms the pathologies which modern states seem to share – especially that of atomization of the citizenry – and the common stories which serve to enact these pathologies.

In the first section of this chapter, I will begin by telling the Christian story of creation, fall, and redemption – as interpreted by Paul, John, and various patristic writers – as the loss and regaining of a primal unity. In the second section, I will then offer a reading of Hobbes, Locke, and Rousseau as attempts to save humanity from the pernicious effects of disunity through the mechanism of the state. In the third section, I will dissect the myth of the 'Wars of Religion,' and argue, in the fourth section, that these wars were not caused by religion but were about the very creation of religion. The fifth section will ask why the state has not saved us, and the final section will argue for a eucharistic counter-politics to that of the state.

I. THE CHRISTIAN STORY

Cain's fratricide, the wickedness of Noah's generation, and the scattering of Babel can only be understood against the backdrop of the natural unity of the human race in the creation story of Genesis 1. The supernatural unity effected in the Body of Christ rests upon a prior natural unity of the whole human race founded on the creation of humankind in the image of God (Gen. 1.27). 'For the divine image does not differ from one individual to another: in all it is the same image,' says Henri de Lubac, summing up patristic anthropology. 'The same mysterious participation in God which causes the soul to exist effects at one and the same time the unity of spirits among themselves.'[2] Such is this unity based on participation in God that, as de Lubac comments, we can no more talk of humans in the plural than we can talk of three Gods. Not individuals but the human race as a whole is created and redeemed. This essential unity in our creation is the natural source of a Church truly Catholic into which all people regardless of nationality are called. Thus Clement of Alexandria:

> This eternal Jesus, the one high priest, intercedes for all and calls on them: 'Hearken,' he cries, 'all you peoples, or rather all you who are endowed with reason, barbarians or Greeks! I summon the whole human race, I who am its author by the will of the Father! Come unto me and gather together as one well-ordered unity under the one God, and under the one Logos of God.'[3]

It is because of this unity that Paul is able to explain to the Romans that 'sin came into the world through one man, and death came through sin, and so death spread to all because all have sinned' (Rom. 5.12). Adam is not merely the first

---

[2] Henri de Lubac, *Catholicism: Christ and the Common Destiny of Man*, trans. Lancelot C. Sheppard and Sister Elizabeth Englund, OCD (San Francisco: Ignatius Press, 1988), p. 29.

[3] Clement of Alexandria, *Protreptic*, c. 12, cited in de Lubac, pp. 32–3.

individual, but represents humanity as a whole.[4] The effect of Adam's disobedience to God, however, is to shatter this created unity. The disruption of the harmonious participation of humanity in God by Adam and Eve's attempted usurpation of God's position – 'when you eat of it your eyes will be opened, and you will be like God' (Gen. 3.5) – is accompanied necessarily by a disruption of human unity, since through the *imago dei* our participation in God is a participation in one another. This disruption begins with Adam's attempt to blame Eve for the sin (3.12). Genesis 4–11 then narrates the effects of the Fall as division and strife; Cain murders Abel, and the 'earth was filled with violence' (6.11). The story of Babel sums up the dynamic of the fall from unity; because of the attempt to usurp God's position, the human race is scattered abroad (Gen. 11.1–9). This sequence of stories is only fully comprehensible against the assumption of a primal unity in the creation story.

In his great work *Catholicism*, de Lubac follows this theme through the writings of the Fathers. Maximus the Confessor sees the Fall as the dispersal of a created unity in which there could be no contradiction between what is mine and what is thine. Cyril of Alexandria writes 'Satan has broken us up.' Augustine pictures Adam almost as if he were a china doll, falling and shattering into pieces which now fill the world.[5] de Lubac comments on these passages and others: 'Instead of trying, as we do almost entirely nowadays, to find within each

---

[4] The view I am developing in this section does not necessarily depend on the historical existence of a single set of biological ancestors, although recent discoveries of 'Eve' and 'Lucy' by anthropologists raise interesting questions about monogenism.

[5] de Lubac, pp. 33–4. In this regard, de Lubac also mentions Origen's dictum 'Where there is sin, there is multiplicity,' but this opposition of unity and multiplicity has possible 'fascist' overtones which are avoided in Paul's account of unity through multiplicity in the Body of Christ.

individual nature what is the hidden blemish and, so to speak, of looking for the mechanical source of the trouble ... these Fathers preferred to envisage the very constitution of the individuals considered as so many cores of natural opposition.'[6] In other words, the effect of sin is the very creation of individuals as such, that is, the creation of an ontological distinction between individual and group.

If sin is scattering into mutual enmity – both between God and humanity and among humans – then redemption will take the form of restoring unity through participation in Christ's Body. The salvation of individuals is only through Christ's salvation of the whole of humanity. Christ is the new Adam because he assumes the whole of humanity. In the incarnation God takes on not simply an individual human body but human nature as such, for, in the slogan of the Alexandrian school, 'that which is not assumed is not saved.' Christ is incorporated in a human body, but likewise humanity is saved by being incorporated into the Body of Christ. The Body of Christ is the locus of mutual participation of God in humanity and humanity in God.

In the Body of Christ as Paul explains it to the Corinthians (1 Cor. 12.4–31), the many are joined into one, but the body continues to consist of many members, each of which is different and not simply interchangeable. Indeed, there is no merely formal equality in the Body of Christ; there are stronger and weaker members, but the inferior members are accorded greater honour (vv. 22–25). Furthermore, the members of the Body are not simply members individually of Christ the Head, but cohere to each other as in a natural body. The members are not 'separate but equal,' but rather participate in each other, such that 'If one member suffers, all

[6] de Lubac, p. 34.

suffer together with it; if one member is honoured, all rejoice together with it' (v. 26).

Incorporation into Christ's Body restores the tarnished image of God in humanity; 'you have put on a new self which will progress towards true knowledge the more it is renewed in the image of its Creator; and in that image there is no room for distinction between Greek and Jew, between the circumcised and uncircumcised, or between barbarian and Scythian, slave and free' (Col. 3.10). Ephesians expresses this in terms of the enmity between Jews and Gentiles: 'For he is our peace; in his flesh he has made both groups into one and has broken down the dividing wall, that is, the hostility between us. He has abolished the law with its commandments and ordinances, that he might create in himself one new humanity in place of the two, thus making peace, and might reconcile both groups to God in one body through the cross, thus putting to death that hostility through it' (Eph. 2.14–16). This reconciliation of Jews and Gentiles is an anticipation of the eschatological gathering of all the nations to Israel, in whom all the nations will be blessed (Gen. 12.3). Jesus dies for the nation, 'and not for the nation only, but also to gather together into one the scattered children of God' (John 11.52).

This eschatological gathering is neither an entirely worldly nor entirely otherworldly event, but blurs the lines between the temporal and the eternal. The individual soul is indeed promised eternal life, but salvation is not merely a matter of the good individual's escape from the violence of the world. We await, rather, a new heaven and a new earth (2 Pet. 3.13; Rev. 21.1), which is already partially present. The heavenly beatific vision is the full consummation of the unification of the human race begun on earth. As Augustine says, 'We are all one in Christ Jesus. And if faith, by which we journey along the way of this life, accomplishes this great wonder, how much more perfectly will the beatific vision bring this unity to fulfillment when we shall see face to face?'[7] In Augustine's vision of the two cities, the reunification of the human race depends on Christians locating true citizenship beyond the confines of the earthly empire. We journey through the *civitas terrena* always aware that our true home is in heaven. This communion with our fellow-citizens in heaven is not, however, an escape from thisworldly politics, but rather a radical interruption of the false politics of the earthly city by the Church. Thus Augustine contrasts the fellowship of the saints in heaven – and on earth – with the violent individualism of the Roman empire, whose virtue is based on a self-aggrandizing *dominium*, the control over what is one's own. It is the Church, uniting earth and heaven, which is the true 'politics.' The earthly city is not a true *res publica* because there can be no justice and no common weal where God is not truly worshipped.[8]

II. THE STATE STORY

The primeval stories told by the classical theorists of the modern state begin from a state of nature. Whether or not this state of nature can be characterized as pre- or post-lapsarian depends on the thinker. Rousseau, not identifiably Christian, assumes an original state of freedom, but is agnostic on the cause of its loss: 'How did this change *from freedom into bondage* come about? I do not know.'[9] Neither Hobbes nor Locke makes any effort to describe a pristine pre-Fall state; both treat of the state of nature as ordained by God, beginning

[7] Augustine, *in Galat. expositio* n. 28, quoted in de Lubac, p. 112.

[8] Augustine, *The City of God*, trans. Marcus Dods (New York: Modern Library, 1950), pp. 686–709 [XIX, 11–28]. See also John Milbank's discussion of Augustine's thought in his *Theology and Social Theory* (Oxford: Blackwell Publishers, 1990), pp. 389–92, 398–411.

[9] Rousseau, p. 2 [Bk 1, ch. 1].

with Adam. For Hobbes, God establishes a system of rewards and punishments, under which Adam's sin would presumably fall. 'The right of nature, whereby God reigneth over men, and punisheth those that break his laws, is to be derived, not from his creating them, as if he required obedience as of gratitude for his benefits; but from his *irresistible power*.'[10] Participation in God is therefore ruled out. As John Milbank has argued, modern politics is founded on the voluntarist replacement of a theology of participation with a theology of will, such that the assumption of humanity into the Trinity by the divine *logos* is supplanted by an undifferentiated God who commands the lesser discrete wills of individual humans by sheer power.[11] The older theology will say that Adam and Eve acted against their true good, which God commands not from sheer will but because God cannot command in any other way than for the good of humanity. In other words, God's will is inseparable from the good. The loss of a theology of participation is therefore a loss of teleology, the intrinsic ends of human life. Hobbes will interpret Adam's dis-obedience as punishable simply because it contradicts God's arbitrary will. Locke too assumes that the state of nature is already characterized by formal mechanisms of will and right, subject to the superior will of God. Thus in the state of nature, each individual is formally discrete and equal, 'unless the lord and master of them all should, by any manifest declaration of his will, set one above another.'[12]

It is important for our purposes to see that this *mythos* establishes human government not on the basis of a primal

[10] Thomas Hobbes, *Leviathan: Or the Matter, Forme, and Power of a Commonwealth Ecclesiasticall and Civil* (New York: Collier Books, 1962), p. 262 [ch. 31].

[11] J. Milbank, *Theology and Social Theory*, pp. 12–15.

[12] John Locke, *Two Treatises of Government* (New York: Dutton, 1924), pp. 118–19 [Bk II, §4].

unity, but on an assumption of the essential individuality of the human race. When Rousseau says that humanity was born free, he primarily means free from one another; by way of contrast, in the Christian interpretation of Genesis, a condition of true human freedom is participation in God with other humans. Hobbes famously posits a natural state of *bellum omnis contra omnem*, which conflict he derives precisely from the formal equality of all human beings,[13] but the more liberal and sanguine Locke agrees on the essential individuality of humanity in the state of nature: 'To understand political power aright, and derive it from its original, we must consider what estate all men are naturally in, and that is, a state of perfect freedom to order their actions, and dispose of their possessions and persons as they think fit, within the bounds of the law of Nature, without asking leave or depending upon the will of any other man'.[14] Hobbes, Rousseau, and Locke all agree that the state of nature is one of individuality; individuals come together on the basis of a social *contract*, each individual entering society in order to protect person and property.

The distinction between mine and thine is therefore inscribed into the modern anthropology. Indeed the early modern theorists of the state depended on a redefinition, according to Roman law, of Adam's *dominium* as sovereignty and power over what is his. As Milbank tells it, *dominium* was traditionally bound up with the ethical management of one's property, and was therefore not a sheer absolute right but was based on ends, namely what was right and just. In Aquinas' thought, Adam's right of property was based on *dominium utile*, justified by its usefulness to society in general. Under the influence of Roman law in the early modern era, the

---

[13] Hobbes, pp. 98–9 [ch. 13].
[14] Locke, p. 118 [Bk II, §4].

Aristotelian suspicion of the right of exchange over use gave way to an absolute right to control one's person and property. This movement was the anthropological complement of the voluntarist theology; humans best exemplify the image of God precisely when exercising sovereignty and unrestricted property rights.[15]

Locke will say, in countering Robert Filmer's deduction of absolute monarchy from Adam, that 'God gave the world to Adam and his posterity in common,'[16] but he then hastens to explain how it is that property is not held communally. This is not the result of some fall from grace, but of God's gift of reason necessary for individuals to derive benefit from the goods of nature. 'Though the earth and all inferior creatures be common to all men, yet every man has a "property" in his own "person." '[17] Individuals appropriate goods from the as-yet-unclaimed abundance of nature and mix their labour or 'person' with it, giving them an exclusive property right to it. According to Locke, God's command to subdue the earth and have dominion over it necessitates the development of private property rights, since it is human labour which both makes nature beneficial to humanity and establishes property as one's own.[18]

Although the essential individualism of the state of nature contrasts with the created unity of the human race found in the Christian interpretation of Genesis 1–2, both accounts agree that salvation is essentially a matter of making peace among competing individuals. It is in soteriology, in other words, that the ends of the Christian *mythos* and the state *mythos* seem to coincide. Hobbes paints this competition

---

[15] Milbank, *Theology and Social Theory*, pp. 12–15.
[16] Locke, *Two Treatises of Government*, p. 129 [Bk II, §25].
[17] Locke, p. 130 [Bk II, §27].
[18] Locke, p. 132 [Bk II, §32–34].

among individuals in the starkest terms: two people in the
state of nature, by nature equal, will want what only one can
have. From the natural equality of humans therefore arises
the war of all against all, from which Leviathan – enacted by
social contract – saves us. Rousseau denies that humans are
'natural enemies;'[19] Locke distinguishes between the state of
nature and a state of war.[20] Nevertheless, both Rousseau and
Locke agree with Hobbes that individuals are compelled into
the social contract by the need to defend one's property and
person from encroachment by other individuals. According to
Locke, 'the pravity of mankind being such that they had
rather injuriously prey upon the fruits of other men's labours
than take pains to provide for themselves' obliges individuals
to enter into society with one another.[21] For Rousseau, the
social contract comes from the need 'to defend and protect,
with all the collective might, the person and property of each
associate.' The state of nature cannot continue; 'humankind
would perish if it did not change its way of life.'[22]

As in Christian soteriology, salvation from the violence of
conflicting individuals comes through the enacting of a social
body. The metaphor of body is most obvious in Hobbes'
figure of the great Leviathan, the artificial man, the
commonwealth or state, in which sovereignty is the soul,
the magistrates the joints, reward and punishment the nerves,
and '[l]astly, the *pacts* and *covenants*, by which the parts of this
body politic were at first made, set together, and united,
resemble that *fiat*, or the *let us make man*, pronounced by God
in the creation.'[23] Leviathan, then, is the new Adam, this one

[19] Rousseau, p. 9 [Bk I, ch. 4].
[20] Locke, *Two Treatises of Government*, pp. 126–7 [Bk II, §16–19].
[21] John Locke, *A Letter Concerning Toleration* (Indianapolis: Bobbs-Merrill, 1955), p. 47.
[22] Rousseau, p. 13 [Bk I, ch. 6].
[23] Hobbes, p. 19 [author's introduction].

of human creation, which saves us from each other. Although less famously than Hobbes, Rousseau and Locke also employ the metaphor of a social body. For Rousseau, a 'collective moral body' is the result of the social contract, which he characterizes in the following terms: 'Each of us puts into the common pool, and under the sovereign control of the general will, his person and all his power. And we, as a community, take each member unto ourselves as an indivisible part of the whole.'[24] Locke deduces his argument for majority rule by employing the metaphor of body, for once the consent of each individual has produced a body, 'it being one body, must move one way,' and that way is 'whither the greater force carries it.'[25]

III. THE WARS OF RELIGION

Thus far I have been treating the Christian story and the state story as parallel accounts of salvation. The soteriology of the modern state is incomprehensible, however, apart from the fact that the Church is perhaps the primary thing from which the modern state is meant to save us. The modern secular state, after all, is founded precisely, the story goes, on the need to keep peace between contentious religious factions. The modern state arose out of the 'Wars of Religion' of the sixteenth and seventeenth centuries, in which the conflicts inherent in civil society, and religion in particular, are luridly displayed. The story is a simple one. When the religious consensus of civil society was shattered by the Reformation, the passions excited by religion as such were loosed, and Catholics and the newly-minted Protestants began killing each other in the name of doctrinal loyalties. 'Transubstan-

---

[24] Rousseau, p. 15 [Bk I, ch. 6].
[25] Locke, *Two Treatises of Government*, p. 165 [Bk II, §96].

tiation, I say!' shouts the Catholic, jabbing his pike at the Lutheran heretic. 'Consubstantiation, damn you!' responds the Lutheran, firing a volley of lead at the papist deviant. The modern secular state and the privatization of religion was necessary, therefore, to keep the peace among warring religious factions.

This fable is a favorite of contemporary liberal political theorists.[26] In Judith Shklar's words

> liberalism ... was born out of the cruelties of the religious civil wars, which forever rendered the claims of Christian charity a rebuke to all religious institutions and parties. If the faith was to survive at all, it would do so privately. The alternative then set, and still before us, is not one between classical virtue and liberal self-indulgence, but between cruel military and moral repression and violence, and a self-restraining tolerance that fences in the powerful to protect the freedom and safety of every citizen ...[27]

According to Jeffrey Stout, the multiplication of religions following on the Reformation produced appeals to incompatible authorities that could not be resolved rationally. Therefore 'liberal principles were the right ones to adopt when competing religious beliefs and divergent conceptions of the good embroiled Europe in the religious wars ... Our early modern ancestors were right to secularize public discourse in the interest of minimizing the ill effects of religious disagreement.'[28]

---

[26] See, for example, John Rawls, 'Justice as Fairness: Political not Metaphysical,' *Philosophy & Public Affairs* (Summer 1985), p. 225; Judith Shklar, *Ordinary Vices* (Cambridge, MA: Harvard University Press, 1984), p. 5; Jeffrey Stout, *The Flight from Authority: Religion, Morality, and the Quest for Autonomy* (Notre Dame, IN: University of Notre Dame Press, 1981), p. 13, 235–42.

[27] Shklar, p. 5.

[28] Stout, p. 241.

I will show that this story puts the matter backwards. The 'Wars of Religion' were not the events that necessitated the birth of the modern state; they were in fact themselves the birthpangs of the state. These wars were not simply a matter of conflict between 'Protestantism' and 'Catholicism,' but were fought largely for the aggrandizement of the emerging state over the decaying remnants of the medieval ecclesial order. It is not merely that political and economic factors played a central role in these wars, nor are we justified in making a facile reduction of religion to more mundane concerns. Rather, to call these conflicts 'Wars of Religion' is an anachronism, for what was at issue in these wars was the very creation of religion as a set of privately held beliefs without direct political relevance. The creation of religion was necessitated by the new state's need to secure absolute sovereignty over its subjects. I hope to challenge the soteriology of the modern state as peacemaker, and show that Christian resistance to state violence depends on a recovery of the Church's resources of resistance.

In the medieval period, the term *status* had been used either in reference to the condition of the ruler (*status principis*), or in the general sense of the condition of the realm (*status regni*). With Machiavelli we begin to see the transition to a more abstract sense of the state as an independent political entity, but only in the works of sixteenth-century French and English humanists does there emerge the modern idea of the state as 'a form of public power separate from both ruler and the ruled, and constituting the supreme political authority within a certain defined territory.'[29] In the medieval period the Church was the supreme common power; the civil authority, as John Figgis put it, was 'the police department of the

[29] Quentin Skinner, *The Foundations of Modern Political Thought* (Cambridge: Cambridge University Press, 1978), vol. II, p. 353.

Church.'[30] The net result of the conflicts of the sixteenth and seventeenth centuries was to invert the dominance of the ecclesiastical over the civil authorities through the creation of the modern state. The chief promoters of this transposition, as Figgis makes plain, 'were Martin Luther and Henry VIII and Philip II, who in reality worked together despite their apparent antagonism.'[31]

It is important to see that the origins of civil dominance over the Church predated the so-called 'Wars of Religion.' As early as the fourteenth century, the controversy between the Papalists and Conciliarists had given rise to quite new developments in the configuration of civil power. Marsilius of Padua had argued that the secular authorities had sole right to the use of coercive force. Indeed, he contended that coercive force by its very nature was secular, and so the Church could be understood only as a moral, and not a jurisdictional, body.[32] Luther took up this argument in his 1523 treatise *Temporal Authority: to what Extent it Should be Obeyed*. Every Christian, Luther maintained, is simultaneously subject to two kingdoms or two governances, the spiritual and the temporal. Coercive power is ordained by God but is given only to the secular powers in order that civil peace be maintained among sinners. Since coercive power is defined as secular, the Church is left with a purely suasive authority, that of preaching the Word of God.[33]

Luther rightly saw that the Church had become worldly

[30] John Neville Figgis, *From Gerson to Grotius, 1414–1625* (New York: Harper Torchbook, 1960), p. 5.

[31] Figgis, p. 6.

[32] Marsilius of Padua, *Defensor Pacis*, trans. Alan Gewirth (Toronto: University of Toronto Press, 1980), pp. 113–26.

[33] Martin Luther, *Temporal Authority: to what Extent it Should be Obeyed*, trans. J. J. Schindel in *Luther's Works*, vol. 45 (Philadelphia: Fortress Press, 1962), pp. 75–129.

and perversely associated with the wielding of the sword. His
intention was to prevent the identification of any politics with
the will of God, and thus extricate the Church from its
entanglement in coercive power.[34] In sanctifying that power
to the use of secular government, however, Luther contributed to the myth of the state as peacemaker which would
be invoked to confine the Church. While apparently
separating civil and ecclesiastical jurisdictions, the effect of
Luther's arguments was in fact to deny any separate
jurisdiction to the Church. Luther writes in *To the Christian
Nobility of the German Nation*, 'I say therefore that since the
temporal power is ordained of God to punish the wicked and
protect the good, it should be left free to perform its office in
the whole body of Christendom without restriction and
without respect to persons, whether it affects pope, bishops,
priests, monks, nuns or anyone else.'[35] Christ has not two
bodies, one temporal and one spiritual, but only one.

The Lutheran doctrine of the two kingdoms signifies,
therefore, the defeat of the medieval metaphor of the two
swords. The entire edifice of ecclesiastical courts and canon
law is eliminated. As Quentin Skinner puts it, 'The idea of the
Pope and Emperor as parallel and universal powers
disappears, and the independent jurisdictions of the *sacerdo-
tium* are handed over to the secular authorities.'[36] The Church
will in time become merely a *congregatio fidelium*, a collection of
the faithful for the purpose of nourishing the faith. What is left
to the Church is increasingly the purely interior government

---

[34] Uwe Siemon-Netto argues this in 'Luther Vilified – Luther
Vindicated,' *Lutheran Forum*, vol. 27 (1993), no. 2, pp. 33–9 and no. 3,
pp. 42–9.
[35] Martin Luther, *To the Christian Nobility of the German Nation*, trans.
Charles M. Jacobs in *Three Treatises* (Philadelphia: Fortress Press, 1966), p.
15.
[36] Skinner, vol. II, p. 15.

of the souls of its members; their bodies are handed over to the secular authorities.

It is not difficult to appreciate the advantages of this view of the Church to the princes of Luther's time. It is important to note, however, that the usurpation of papal perquisites in the first half of the sixteenth century was not limited to those princes who had embraced Protestantism. The Catholic princes of Germany, the Habsburgs of Spain and the Valois of France all twisted the Pope's arm, extracting concessions that considerably increased their control over the Church within their realms. As Richard Dunn points out, 'Charles V's soldiers sacked Rome, not Wittenberg, in 1527.'[37] When Charles V, Holy Roman Emperor, finally turned his attention to the Protestants in 1547, igniting the first major War of Religion, his attack on the Lutheran states was an attempt to consolidate imperial authority rather than an expression of doctrinal zealotry. This fact was not lost on the princes, both Catholic and Protestant, whose power was growing in opposition to that of the Habsburgs and the Church. When in 1552–53 the Lutheran princes (aided by the French Catholic King Henry II) defeated the imperial forces, the German Catholic princes stood by, neutral.[38] The war ended in 1555 with the Peace of Augsburg, which allowed the temporal authority of each political unit to choose either Lutheranism or Catholicism for its realm: *cuius regio, eius religio*.

---

[37] Richard S. Dunn, *The Age of Religious Wars: 1559–1689* (New York: W. W. Norton & Company, 1970), p. 6. Dunn adds that 'when the papacy belatedly sponsored a reform program, both the Habsburgs and the Valois refused to endorse much of it, rejecting especially those Trentine decrees which encroached on their sovereign authority. In refusing to cooperate with Rome, the Catholic princes checked papal ambitions to restore the Church's medieval political power.'

[38] Dunn, pp. 48–9.

Historians often claim that the Reformation and Counter-Reformation retarded the secularizing trend toward the modern state by making politics theological. It is certain that both reformers and their Catholic adversaries in the sixteenth century agreed that the idea of the state should include upholding the true religion. This in itself was, however, a radical departure from the medieval idea of the proper ordering of civilization. Pre-sixteenth century Christendom assumed, at least in theory, that the civil and ecclesiastical powers were different departments of the same body, with the ecclesiastical hierarchy of course at the head. The sixteenth century maintained the conception of a single body, but inverted the relationship, setting the good prince to rule over the Church. The eventual elimination of the Church from the public sphere was prepared by the dominance of the princes over the Church in the sixteenth century.

The policy of *cuius regio, eius religio* was more than just a sensible compromise to prevent bloodshed among the people, now divided by commitment to different faiths. It was in fact a recognition of the dominance of secular rulers over the Church, to the extent that the faith of a people was controlled by and large by the desires of the prince. G. R. Elton puts it bluntly: 'The Reformation maintained itself wherever the lay power (prince or magistrates) favoured it; it could not survive where the authorities decided to suppress it.'[39] There is a direct relationship between the success of efforts to restrict supra-national Church authority and the failure of the Reformation within those realms. In other words, wherever concordats between the Papacy and temporal rulers had already limited the jurisdiction of the Church within national boundaries, there the princes saw no need to throw off the yoke of Catholicism, precisely because Catholicism had

[39] G. R. Elton, 'The Age of the Reformation,' quoted in Dunn, p. 6.

already been reduced, to a greater extent, to a merely suasive body under the heel of the secular power. In France the Pragmatic Sanction of Bourges had accomplished this in 1438, eliminating papal collection of the Annate tax, taking away the Pope's right to nominate candidates for vacant sees, and giving the crown the formerly papal prerogative of supplicating in favour of aspirants to most benefices. The Concordat of Bologna in 1516 confirmed the French kings' control over Church appointments and revenues. In Spain the crown was granted even wider concessions between 1482 and 1508. France and Spain remained Catholic. Where such concordats were not arranged, as in England, Germany, and Scandinavia, conflicts between the Church and the secular rulers – which, it must be remembered, predated Luther – contributed significantly in every case to the success of the Reformation.[40]

After the Concordat of Bologna, the French kings and Catherine de Medici saw no advantage to the Reformation in France. The early settlement of civil dominance over the Church was a crucial factor in the building of a strong, centralized monarchy during the rule of Francis I from 1515 to 1547. When Calvinism began to challenge the ecclesiastical system in France, it therefore formed a threat to royal power. The rising bourgeoisie in provincial towns, anxious to combat centralized control, joined the Huguenots in large numbers. Moreover, as many as two-fifths of the nobility rallied to the Calvinist cause. They wanted to reverse the trend toward absolute royal authority and coveted power like that of the German princes to control the Church in their own lands.[41]

For the main instigators of the carnage, doctrinal loyalties were at best secondary to their stake in the rise or defeat of the

---

[40] Skinner, vol. II, pp. 59–60.
[41] Dunn, p. 24. See also Skinner, vol. II, pp. 254–9.

centralized state. Both Huguenot and Catholic noble factions plotted for control of the monarchy. The Queen Mother Catherine de Medici, for her part, attempted to bring both factions under the sway of the crown. At the Colloquy of Poissy in 1561, Catherine proposed bringing Calvinist and Catholic together under a state-controlled Church modelled on Elizabeth's Church of England. Catherine had no particular theological scruples and was therefore stunned to find that both Catholic and Calvinist ecclesiologies prevented such an arrangement. Eventually Catherine decided that statecraft was more satisfying than theology, and, convinced that the Huguenot nobility were gaining too much influence over the king, she unleashed the infamous 1572 St Bartholomew's Day massacre of thousands of Protestants. After years of playing Protestant and Catholic factions off one another, Catherine finally threw in her lot with the Catholic Guises. She would attempt to wipe out the Huguenot leadership and thereby quash the Huguenot nobility's influence over king and country.[42]

The St Bartholomew's Day massacre was the last time it was easy to sort out the Catholics from the Protestants in the French civil wars. By 1576 both Protestant and Catholic nobles were in rebellion against King Henry III. In that year was formed the Catholic League, whose stated goal was 'to restore to the provinces and estates of this kingdom the rights, privileges, franchises and ancient liberties such as they were in the time of King Clovis, the first Christian king.'[43] The League wished to check the power of the crown by appealing to the medieval doctrine of sovereignty, in which kingship was based on the will of the people. The Catholic League was

[42] Dunn, pp. 23–6.
[43] Quoted in Franklin C. Palm, *Calvinism and the Religious Wars* (New York: Henry Holt and Company, 1932), pp. 54–5.

opposed by another Catholic party, the *Politiques*, who pushed for an absolutist vision of the state. For the *Politiques* the state was an end in itself which superseded all other interests, and the monarch held absolute sovereignty by divine right. They advocated a Gallican Catholic Church and liberty of conscience in the private exercise of religion. Most *Politiques* allied themselves with the Protestants following the formation of the Catholic League.[44]

Ecclesial loyalties were complicated further by the entrance into the fray of Spain's Philip II, who wanted to place a Spanish infanta on the French throne. Philip financed the Guises' attack on Paris in 1588, thus compelling the Catholic King Henry III to ally himself with the Protestants under Henry of Navarre. Upon the King's death in 1589, Henry of Navarre took the throne as Henry IV, and conveniently converted to Catholicism four years later. The war ended in 1598 when Philip II finally gave up Spanish designs on the French throne.[45]

The end of the French civil wars is seen as the springboard for the development of the absolutist vision of sovereign power unchallenged within the state which would come to full fruition in seventeenth-century France. It is common to maintain that a strong centralized power was necessary to rescue the country from the anarchy of violence produced by religious fervour. My brief sketch of these wars should make clear that such a view is problematic. The rise of a centralized bureaucratic state *preceded* these wars and was based on the fifteenth-century assertion of civil dominance over the Church in France. At issue in these wars was not simply Catholic versus Protestant, transubstantiation versus spiritual presence. The Queen Mother who unleashed the massacre of St

---

[44] Palm, pp. 51–4.
[45] Dunn, pp. 27–31.

Bartholomew's Day was not a religious zealot but a thoroughgoing *Politique* with a stake in stopping the nobility's challenge to royal pretensions toward absolute power.[46]

In the seventeenth century, the success of the French example of a centralized state was not lost on the Holy Roman Emperor, who had long wished to make his nominal power real over the lesser princes. The result was the Thirty Years' War (1618–1648), the bloodiest of the so-called 'Wars of Religion.' Emperor Ferdinand II's goal was to consolidate his patchwork empire into a modern state: Habsburg, Catholic, and ruled by one sovereign, unrivalled authority. To accomplish this Ferdinand relied on shifting alliances with lesser princes, mercenary soldiers, and his Spanish Habsburg cousins. Again, ecclesial loyalties were not easy to sort out. On the one hand, Ferdinand relied on the Lutheran elector of Saxony to help reconquer Bohemia, and his troops were commanded by the Bohemian Protestant soldier of fortune, Albrecht von Wallenstein. On the other hand, the Catholic petty princes opposed Ferdinand's attempts to centralize his power and his neglect of the imperial Diet.[47]

The war's tide turned against Ferdinand in 1630 when Sweden's Gustavus Adolphus entered the conflict against him. Sweden's effect on the war was great, in large part because France under Cardinal Richelieu had decided to subsidize an army of 36,000 Swedes in German territory. Presumably the Catholic Cardinal was not motivated by love of Luther to support the Protestant cause. France's interest lay in keeping the Habsburg empire fragmented, and France's interest superseded that of her Church. In 1635

---

[46] See J. H. M. Salmon, *Society in Crisis: France in the Sixteenth Century* (London and Tonbridge: Ernest Benn Limited, n.d.), pp. 189–90. After the massacre a flood of Huguenot literature explored the influence of Machiavellianism on the Queen Mother's actions.

[47] Dunn, pp. 69–73.

the French sent troops, and the last thirteen years of the war –
the bloodiest – were essentially a struggle between the
Habsburgs and the Bourbons, the two great Catholic
dynasties of Europe.[48]

IV. THE CREATION OF RELIGION

Historians of this period commonly point out that religious
motives are not the only ones at work in fuelling these wars.
As J. H. Elliot comments, whether or not these are in fact
'Wars of Religion' depends on whether you ask a Calvinist
pastor, a peasant, or a prince of this period.[49] The point I
wish to make, however, goes beyond questions of sincerity of
personal religious conviction. What is at issue behind these
wars is the creation of 'religion' as a set of beliefs which is
defined as personal conviction and which can exist separately
from one's public loyalty to the state. The creation of religion,
and thus the privatization of the Church, is correlative to the
rise of the state. It is important therefore to see that the
principal promoters of the wars in France and Germany were
in fact not pastors and peasants, but kings and nobles with a
stake in the outcome of the movement toward the centralized,
hegemonic state.

In the medieval period, the term *religio* is used very
infrequently. When it appears it most commonly refers to the

---

[48] Dunn, pp. 73–8.

[49] J. H. Elliot, *Europe Divided: 1559–1598* (New York: Harper & Row,
1968), p. 108. Elliot quotes the words of the sixteenth-century Venetian
ambassador as to the secular motivation behind the French civil wars: 'In
like manner as Caesar would have no equal and Pompey no superior, these
civil wars are born of the wish of the cardinal of Lorraine to have no equal,
and the Admiral (Coligny) and the house of Montmorency to have no
superior.'

monastic life. As an adjective the 'religious' are those who belong to an order, as distinguished from lay Christians or 'secular' clergy. When 'religion' enters the English language, it retains these meanings and refers to the life of a monastery or order. Thus around 1400 the 'religions of England' are the various orders.[50]

Thomas Aquinas devotes only one question of the *Summa Theologiae* to *religio*; it names a virtue that directs a person to God. St Thomas says that religion does not differ essentially from sanctity. It differs logically, however, in that religion refers specifically to the liturgical practices of the Church. Thus, according to St Thomas, 'The word religion is usually used to signify the activity by which man gives the proper reverence to God through actions which specifically pertain to divine worship, such as sacrifice, oblations, and the like.'[51] In response to the query 'Does religion have any external actions?,' Thomas answers affirmatively and emphasizes the unity of body and soul in the worship of God.[52] As a virtue, *religio* is a habit, knowledge embodied in the disciplined actions of the Christian. In Aquinas' view virtuous actions do not proceed from rational principles separable from the agent's particular history; virtuous persons instead are embedded in communal practices of habituation of body and soul that give their lives direction to the good.[53]

Religio for St Thomas is just one virtue that presupposes a context of ecclesial practices which are both communal and particular to the Christian Church. Wilfred Cantwell Smith notes that during the Middle Ages, considered by moderns

[50] Wilfred Cantwell Smith, *The Meaning and End of Religion* (New York: The Macmillan Company, 1962), p. 31.

[51] St Thomas Aquinas, *Summa Theologiae*, ed. Blackfriars (New York: McGraw-Hill, 1964), II-II.81.8.

[52] St Thomas Aquinas, II-II.81.7.

[53] St Thomas Aquinas, I-II.49–55.

the 'most religious' period of Christian history, no one ever thought to write a book on religion.[54] In fact he suggests that 'the rise of the concept "religion" is in some ways correlated with a decline in the practice of religion itself.'[55] In other words the rise of the modern concept of religion is associated with the decline of the Church as the particular locus of the communal practice of *religio*.

The dawn of the modern concept of religion occurs around the late fifteenth century, first appearing in the work of the Italian Renaissance figure Marsilio Ficino. His 1474 work entitled *De Christiana Religione* is the first to present *religio* as a universal human impulse common to all. In Ficino's Platonic scheme, *religio* is the ideal of genuine perception and worship of God. The various historical manifestations of this common impulse, the varieties of pieties and rites that we now call religions, are all just more or less true (or untrue) representations of the one true *religio* implanted in the human heart. Insofar as it becomes a universal impulse, religion is thus interiorized and removed from its particular ecclesial context.[56]

The second major shift in the meaning of the term religion, which takes shape through the late sixteenth and seventeenth centuries, is toward religion as a system of beliefs. Religion moves from a virtue to a set of propositions. Political theorist Hugo Grotius, in his *De Veritate Religionis Christianae*, can therefore write that the Christian religion teaches, rather than simply is, the true worship of God. At the same time the plural 'religions' arises, an impossibility under the medieval usage.[57]

---

54 Cantwell Smith, p. 32.
55 Cantwell Smith, p. 19.
56 Cantwell Smith, pp. 32–4.
57 Cantwell Smith, pp. 32–44.

In sixteenth-century France, *Politiques* and humanists began to provide a theoretical reconfiguration of Christianity that fitted it into the generic category of 'religion.' In his 1544 work *The Concord of the World*, Guillaume Postel provided an argument in favour of religious liberty based on the construal of Christianity as a set of demonstrable moral truths, rather than theological claims and practices which take a particular social form called the Church. Christianity, according to Postel, is based on common, universal truths which underlie all particular expressions of 'religious belief.' Liberty of conscience in matters of 'religion' is essential because all rational people are able to recognize these universal truths.[58]

The *Politique* political theorist Jean Bodin also advocates liberty of conscience in religion as part and parcel of a plan for an absolutist state with a centralized sovereign authority. In his landmark *Six Books of the Commonwealth* (1576), religion is treated under the heading 'How Seditions may be Avoided.' 'Even atheists agree,' according to Bodin, 'that nothing so tends to the preservation of commonwealths as religion, since it is the force that at once secures the authority of kings and governors, the execution of the laws, the obedience of subjects, reverence for the magistrates, fear of ill-doing, and knits each and all in the bonds of friendship.'[59] Religion for Bodin is a generic concept; he states directly that he is not concerned with which form of religion is best. The people should be free in conscience to choose whichever religion they desire. What is important is that once a form of religion has been embraced by a people, the sovereign must forbid any public dispute over religious matters to break out and thereby threaten his authority. Bodin cites with approval

[58] Skinner, vol. II, pp. 244–6.
[59] Jean Bodin, *Six Books of the Commonwealth*, trans. and abr. M. J. Tooley (Oxford: Basil Blackwell, n.d.), p. 141.

some German towns' prohibition of 'all discussion of religion' on pain of death after the Peace of Augsburg. Religious diversity is to be allowed only where it is too costly for the sovereign to suppress it.[60]

The concept of religion being born here is one of domesticated belief systems which are, insofar as it is possible, to be manipulated by the sovereign for the benefit of the state. Religion is no longer a matter of certain bodily practices within the Body of Christ, but is limited to the realm of the 'soul,' and the body is handed over to the state. John Figgis puts it this way:

> The rise and influence of the *Politiques* was the most notable sign of the times at the close of the sixteenth century. The existence of the party testifies to the fact that for many minds the religion of the State has replaced the religion of the Church, or, to be more correct, that religion is becoming individual while the civil power is recognized as having the paramount claims of an organized society upon the allegiance of its members. What Luther's eminence as a religious genius partially concealed becomes more apparent in the *Politiques*; for the essence of their position is to treat the unity of the State as the paramount end, to which unity in religion must give way.[61]

Among the founders of the modern state, no one is more blunt than Thomas Hobbes in bringing religion to the service of the sovereign. He defines religion as a binding impulse that suggests itself to humans in the natural condition of their ignorance and fear. 'Gnawed on by fear of death, poverty, or other calamity,'[62] and unaware of secondary causes, there

[60] Bodin, pp. 140–2.
[61] Figgis, p. 124.
[62] Hobbes, p. 88.

develops in all parts of the globe a belief in powers invisible, and a natural devotion to what is feared. Some worship according to their own inventions, others according to the command of the true God Himself through supernatural revelation. But the leaders of both kinds of religions have arranged their devotions 'to make those men that relied on them, the more apt to obedience, laws, peace, charity, and civil society.'[63] Religion for Hobbes derives from fear and need of security, the very same root from which springs the social contract and commonwealth. Where God has planted religion through revelation, therefore, there also has God established a 'peculiar kingdom,' the Kingdom of God, a polity in which there is no distinction of spiritual and temporal. The 'Kingdom' of God is no mere metaphor; by it is meant the commonwealth, ruled over by one sovereign who is both 'ecclesiasticall and civil.'[64]

Hobbes' aim in uniting Church and state is peace. Without universal obedience to but one sovereign, civil war between temporal and spiritual powers is tragically inevitable.[65] Its inevitability lies in Hobbes' ontology of violence. The war of all against all is the natural condition of humankind. It is cold fear and need for security, the foundation of both religion and the social contract, that drives humans from their nasty and brutish circumstances and into the arms of Leviathan. This soteriology of the state as peacemaker demands that its sovereign authority be absolutely alone and without rival.

In Hobbes it is not so much that the Church has been subordinated to the civil power; Leviathan has rather swallowed the Church whole in its yawning maw. Scripture is nothing less than the law of the commonwealth, such that

[63] Hobbes, p. 90.
[64] Hobbes, pp. 94, 297–9.
[65] Hobbes, pp. 340–1.

the interpretation of Scripture is the responsibility of the sovereign. The Christian king is supreme pastor of his realm, and has power to preach, to baptize, to administer the eucharist, and even to ordain.[66] The sovereign is not only priest but prophet; the king reserves the right to police all charism and censor any public prophecy. The 'private man,' because 'thought is free,' is at liberty in his heart to think what he will, provided in public he exercise his right to remain silent.[67] In a Christian commonwealth, Hobbes denies even the theoretical possibility of martyrdom, since he defines martyrs as only those who die publicly proclaiming the simple doctrine 'Jesus is the Christ.' A Christian sovereign would never impede such a simple (and contentless) profession of faith. As for other more specific doctrines or practices for which a Christian might die, these could only go under the title 'subversion,' never martyrdom, since the sovereign has the sole right to determine proper Christian practice and sanction any public deviations therefrom. Those Christians who find themselves under a heathen regime Hobbes counsels to obey, even unto public apostasy, provided they maintain the faith in their hearts, since Christian faith is wholly interior and not subject to external coercion.[68]

'A Church,' Hobbes writes, 'is the same thing with a civil commonwealth, consisting of Christian men; and is called a *civil state*.'[69] It follows, therefore, that there is no one Church universal, but only as many Churches as there are Christian states, since there is no power on earth to which the

---

[66] Hobbes, pp. 395–8. In chapter 42 of *Leviathan* Hobbes provides a lengthy explanation of why sovereigns have this power without needing to bother with such inconveniences as apostolic succession and the imposition of hands.

[67] Hobbes, p. 324.

[68] Hobbes, pp. 363–6.

[69] Hobbes, p. 340.

commonwealth is subject. The transnational Church produces conflict by dividing people's loyalties between sovereign
and pontiff; 'there must needs follow faction and civil war in
the commonwealth, between the *Church* and *State*.'[70] Absolute
unity of Church and state is therefore necessary to emerge
fully from the state of nature and into the peaceful embrace of
Leviathan. 'Religion' therefore becomes a means of binding
the individual to the sovereign. Hobbes contends that the
members of a Church are bound as in a natural body, but not
to one another, for each one depends only on the sovereign.[71]
The Body of Christ is thereby severely nominalized, scattered
and absorbed into the body of the state.

Rousseau has a similar concern for the unity of the state. He
asks why the pagan world had no 'religious wars.' The answer
is that each state had its own religions and its own gods.
Rather than produce division, Rousseau argues, such an
arrangement meant that the gods of one nation had no power
over the people of another nation, and therefore the gods were
not imperialist or jealous. The Romans eventually adopted the
wise policy of tolerating the gods of vanquished peoples, and
so paganism in the Roman empire could be considered a
'single, homogeneous religion' despite the diversity of gods and
religions. 'Thus matters stood when Jesus made his appear-
ance, bent on establishing a spiritual kingdom on earth – an
enterprise which forced a wedge between the political system
and the theological system, and so undermined the unity of
the state. Hence the internal divisions that – *as we are about to
see* – have never ceased to plague the Christian peoples.'[72]
Christianity produces divisions within the state body precisely
because it has pretensions to be a body which transcends state

[70] Hobbes, pp. 340–1.
[71] Hobbes, p. 418.
[72] Rousseau, p. 151 [Bk IV, ch. 8].

boundaries. 'What makes the clergy a body ... [is] communion among churches. Communication and excommunication
– these are the clergy's social compact.' Priests in communion
are 'fellow-citizens' even though they come from different
parts of the globe.[73] This system, 'so obviously baneful'
precisely because it 'impairs social unity,' must be remedied by
the creation of a civil religion to bind the citizen to the state.
Although Rousseau congratulates Hobbes for clearly diagnos-
ing both the problem and the cure to the Church question,
Rousseau insists on the tolerance of a diversity of religions,
provided they have to do only with the 'purely inward
worship' of God, do not interfere with the duties of citizens to
the state, and tolerate other religions. Intolerant religions such
as Roman Catholicism are not to be tolerated.[74]

In Locke we find a more recognizable form of liberal
tolerance, but it is essential to see the fundamental agreement
between Hobbes, Rousseau, and Locke on the need to
domesticate the Body of Christ in order to produce unity.
Locke's concern, again, is the division produced by the 'Wars
of Religion' which have plagued England and the Continent.

> I esteem it above all things necessary to distinguish
> exactly the business of civil government from that of
> religion ... If this be not done, there can be no end put
> to the controversies that will be always arising between
> those that have, or at least pretend to have, on the one
> side, a concernment for the interest of men's souls, and,
> on the other side, a care of the commonwealth. The
> commonwealth seems to me to be a society of men
> constituted only for the procuring, preserving, and
> advancing their own civil interests.[75]

---

[73] Rousseau, p. 153 [Bk IV, ch. 8].
[74] Rousseau, pp. 153–62 [Bk IV, ch. 8].
[75] Locke, *A Letter Concerning Toleration*, p. 17.

Hobbes and Bodin both prefer religious uniformity for reasons of state, but it is important to see that once Christians are made to chant 'We have no king but Caesar,' it is really a matter of indifference to the sovereign whether there be one religion or many. Once the state has succeeded in establishing dominance over, or absorbing, the Church, it is but a small step from absolutist enforcement of religious unity to the toleration of religious diversity. In other words, there is a logical progression from Bodin and Hobbes to Locke.[76] Lockean liberalism can afford to be gracious toward 'religious pluralism' precisely because 'religion' as an interior matter is the state's own stepchild. Locke says that the state cannot coerce the religious conscience because of the irreducibly solitary nature of religious judgement; 'All the life and power of true religion consist in the inward and full persuasion of the mind.'[77] But for the very same reason he categorically denies the social nature of the Church, which is redefined as a free association of like-minded individuals.[78]

Toleration ironically becomes the tool through which the Church is divided and conquered. Locke's ideas were enshrined in England's Toleration Act of 1689, drawing an end to what is considered the 'Age of Religious Wars.'[79]

---

[76] John Milbank also points to the kinship of modern absolutism and modern liberalism in slightly different terms. 'It is precisely the formal character of state power as guaranteeing personal security and non-interference in "private" pursuits (selling, contracts, education, choice of abode) which demands that this power be otherwise unlimited and absolutely alone. Hobbes was simply more clear-sighted than later apparently more "liberal" thinkers like Locke in realizing that a liberal peace requires a single undisputed power, but not necessarily a continued majority consensus, which may not be forthcoming.' Milbank, *Theology and Social Theory*, p. 13.

[77] Locke, *A Letter Concerning Toleration*, p. 18.

[78] Locke, *A Letter Concerning Toleration*, p. 35.

[79] Although William of Orange has often been presented as a religious zealot, fervent Calvinist and scourge of papists, recent scholarship makes

Catholics, of course, were explicitly excluded from the Toleration Act, not simply because of what we would call 'religious bigotry,' but because the Catholics in England had as yet refused to define themselves as a 'religion' at all. The English Catholics continued to regard the Church as a transnational body, and did not yet fully accept that the state had won.

Perhaps the best way to get a flavour for the 'religious' wars of the seventeenth century is to read the words of one of the interested parties. The following is from a 1685 English anti-Catholic tract penned by the Earl of Clarendon:

> No man was ever truly and really angry (otherwise than the warmth and multiplication of words in the dispute produced it) with a man who believed *Transubstantiation* ...; but when he will for the support of this *Paradox* introduce an authority for the imperious determination thereof ... it is no wonder if passion breaks in at this door, and kindles a Fire strong enough to consume the House. This is the Hinge upon which all the other

cont.
him out to be a 'thoroughgoing *politique*' for whom theology was but a tool of statecraft. On the eve of the Glorious Revolution, William and the Dutch States General embarked on a lobbying campaign aimed at convincing Catholic Europe that they had no Protestant motives for invading England, and that Catholic worship would be protected. The Dutch were on the brink of war with France, and were convinced that their chances of winning hinged on turning the English against the French. At the same time, French propagandists sought to paint the conflict as a *guerre de religion*, not a *guerre d'état*. At least one English pamphleteer thought that interpretation unlikely, writing in 1688 'none that know the religion of the Hollander would judge the Prince or States would be at the charge of a dozen fly-boats or herring busses to propagate it.' See Jonathan I. Israel, 'William III and Toleration' in *From Persecution to Toleration*, eds. Ole Peter Grell, Jonathan I. Israel, and Nicholas Tyacke (Oxford: Clarendon Press, 1991), pp. 129–42.

controversies between us and the *English* Catholicks do
so intirely hang.[80]

Clearly the Pope can inspire deadly passion in a way that
Eucharistic doctrine cannot because at stake in the conflict is
the loyalty of the Christian to the state; doctrine is being
defined as a matter of internal conscience, not available for
public dispute. Clarendon continues

> Their opinions of *Purgatory* or *Transubstantiation* would
> never cause their *Allegiance* to be suspected, more than
> any other error in Sence, Grammar or Philosophy, if
> those opinions were not instances of their dependance
> upon another Jurisdiction foreign, and inconsistent with
> their duty to the *King*, and destructive to the *peace* of the
> *Kingdom*: and in that sence and Relation the Politick
> Government of the Kingdom takes notice of those
> opinions, which yet are not enquired into or punished
> for themselves.[81]

I do not wish to argue that no Christian ever bludgeoned
another over dogma held dear. What I hope to have shown,
however, is how the dominance of the state over the Church
in the sixteenth and seventeenth centuries allowed temporal
rulers to direct doctrinal conflicts to secular ends. The new
state required unchallenged authority within its borders, and
so the domestication of the Church. Church leaders became
acolytes of the state as the religion of the state replaced that of
the Church, or more accurately, the very concept of religion
as separable from the Church was invented.

---

[80] Earl of Clarendon, *Animadversions upon a Book, Intituled, Fanaticism
Fanatically Imputed to the Catholick Church, by Dr. Stillingfleet, And the Imputation
Refuted and Retorted by S.C.* (London: Rich. Royston, 1685), p. 12.
[81] Earl of Clarendon, p. 11.

V. WHY HAS THE STATE FAILED TO SAVE US?

Liberal theorists would have us believe that the state stepped in like a scolding schoolteacher on the playground of doctrinal dispute to put fanatical religionists in their proper place. Warnings about the dangers of public faith, however, ignore the fact that transfer of ultimate loyalty to the nation-state has only increased the scope of modern warfare. Anthony Giddens has shown how the new sixteenth-century doctrine of the state's absolute sovereignty within a defined territory carried with it an increase in the use of war to expand and consolidate borders. Traditional polities were bounded by frontiers, peripheral regions in which the authority of the centre was thinly spread. The territories of medieval rulers were often not continuous; one prince might own land deep within the territory of another. Furthermore, the residents of a territory might owe varying allegiances to several different nobles, and only nominal allegiance to the king. Only with the emergence of nation-states, according to Giddens, are states circumscribed by borders, known lines demarcating the exclusive domain of sovereign power, especially its monopoly over the means of violence. Attempts to consolidate territory and assert sovereign control often brought about violent conflict. More importantly, borders in the nation-state system include the assumption of a 'state of nature' existing between states which increases the possibility of war.[82] Our fellow-citizens are limited to all those presently

---

[82] Anthony Giddens, *The Nation-State and Violence* (Berkeley: University of California Press, 1987), pp. 50-1, 86-90. Borders imposed by the nation-state system continue to cause conflict. The 1991 Gulf War was largely a product of artificial borders drawn by the British after World War I, which divided the Arab world into artificial and often mutually antagonistic nation-states. The Iraq-Kuwait border was drawn arbitrarily by the British High Commander Percy Cox, deliberately denying newly created Iraq access to the sea in order to keep it dependent on Britain. See Glenn

living Britons, Americans, Germans, etc. The dominance of state soteriology has made it perfectly reasonable to drop cluster bombs on 'foreign' villages, and perfectly unreasonable to dispute 'religious' matters in public.

The state *mythos* is based on a 'theological' anthropology that precludes any truly social process. The recognition of our participation in one another through our creation in the image of God is replaced by the recognition of the other as the bearer of individual rights, which may or may not be given by God, but which serve only to separate what is mine from what is thine. Participation in God and in one another is a threat to the formal mechanism of contract, which assumes that we are *essentially* individuals who enter into relationship with one another only when it is to one's individual advantage to do so. The mechanism of contract is purely 'formal' in the sense that it has no intrinsic relationship to ends – the providential purpose of God – but is definable only as a means. The state can never truly integrate the individual and the group because there is nothing transcending the two-dimensional calculus of individual/aggregate through which individual and group are related.

State soteriology has tried to unify humankind by incorporation into a body of a grotesque sort. Beginning with an anthropology of formally equal individuals guided by no common ends, the best the state can hope to do is to keep these individuals from interfering with each other's rights. While this can serve to mitigate the conflictual effects of individualism, it cannot hope to enact a truly social process. The body that is enacted is a monstrosity of many separate limbs proceeding directly out of a gigantic head. Hobbes

cont.
Frankel, 'Lines in the Sand,' *The Gulf War Reader*, eds. Micah L. Sifry and Christopher Cerf (New York: Times Books, 1991), pp. 16–20.

foresaw this with his usual clarity; in a true commonwealth the members cohere, not as in a natural body to one another, but only to the sovereign.[83] Rousseau too anticipated a perfect panopticon, such that 'each citizen should be completely independent vis-à-vis each of the others, and as dependent as can be vis-à-vis the city.'[84] This arrangement is not an accident of Hobbes' and Rousseau's 'overemphasis' on the state, but proceeds logically from the anthropology of individual *dominium* on which the liberal state is founded. Because of this modern politics is centripetal; talk of '*the* health care debate,' for example, principally means attempts to exert influence over the bureaucratic organs of the state with regard to health care. Rather than 'cohere' directly to one another, we relate to each other through the state by the formal mechanism of contract. Paul's image of the Body – internally differentiated yet suffering and rejoicing as one – is supplanted by a formal interchangeability of each individual with any other.

In the absence of shared ends, individuals relate to each other by means of contract, which assumes a guarantee by force. Hobbes was of course clear on this, but Locke too assumed, as we have seen, that the state body moves in whichever way the greater force compels it. Max Weber rightly perceived that the modern state cannot be defined by ends, but only by its peculiar means, which is a monopoly on the legitimate use of force.[85] Internally, such force is necessary to keep the mass of individuals from interfering with each other's rights. Externally, the violence of war is necessary to provide some unity – albeit a false one – to a society lacking in

---

[83] Hobbes, p. 418 [ch. 42].

[84] Rousseau, p. 58 [Bk II, ch. 12].

[85] Max Weber, 'Politics as a Vocation,' in *From Max Weber: Essays on Sociology*, trans. and ed. H. H. Gerth and C. Wright Mills (New York: Oxford University Press, 1946), pp. 77–8.

any truly social process. As Raymond Williams and others have argued, war is for the liberal state a simulacrum of the social process, the primary mechanism for achieving social integration in a society with no shared ends.[86] In a word, violence becomes the state's *religio*, its habitual discipline for binding us one to another.

Far from coming on the scene as peacekeeper, we have seen that the rise of the state was at the very root of the so-called 'religious' wars, directing with bloodied hands a new secular theatre of absolute power. The wars of the nineteenth and twentieth centuries testify that the transfer of ultimate loyalty to the liberal nation-state has not curbed the toll of war's atrocities. Liberal theorists assume that public faith has a dangerous tendency to violence, and thus preclude the possibility of any truly social Christian ethic. I believe, in contrast, that the Church needs to reclaim the 'political' nature of its faith if it is to resist the violence of the state. What this may mean, however, must go beyond mere strategies to insinuate the Church into the making of public policy. If this book is a plea for the social and political nature of the Christian faith, it is also a plea for a Christian practice that escapes the thrall of the state.

VI. TOWARD A EUCHARISTIC COUNTER-POLITICS

If it is true that the modern state is but a false copy of the Body of Christ, then it should be obvious that state power is the last thing the Church should want. To overcome the privatization of Christianity through attempts, direct or indirect, to influence the state is worse than futile as long as

---

[86] See Raymond Williams, *Towards 2000* (Harmondsworth: Penguin Books, 1985), pp. 218–40.

what is meant by 'politics' remains centripetal. Fortunately, in the making of the Body of Christ, Christians participate in a practice which envisions a proper 'anarchy,' not in the sense that it proposes chaos, but in that it challenges the false order of the state. The Eucharist is the heart of true *religio*, a practice of binding us to the Body of Christ which is our salvation.

The Eucharist defuses both the false theology and the false anthropology of will and right by the stunning 'public' *leitourgia* in which humans are made members of God's very Body. 'Just as the living Father sent me, and I live because of the Father, so whoever eats me will live because of me' (John 6.57). Augustine envisions Jesus saying, 'I am the food of the fully grown; grow and you will feed on me. And you will not change me into you like the food your flesh eats, but you will be changed into me.'[87] The contrast with Locke's explanation of property – that through labour one assimilates things from the state of nature to the property in one's person – is extremely suggestive. Indeed, in the Eucharist the foundational distinction between mine and thine is radically effaced (cf. Acts 2.44–47). Christ's restoration of the *imago dei* in humanity is consummated in individuals in the Eucharist, in which our separateness is overcome precisely by participation in Christ's Body.

The Body of Christ which overcomes the scattering of humanity through Adam's sin is not enacted by any social contract but is always received as a gift; 'the free gift is not like the effect of the one man's sin' (Rom. 5.16). The Eucharist undercuts the primacy of contract and exchange in modern social relations. For, as we have seen, the state enacts the formal interchangeability of the subject, removed from

---

[87] Augustine, *Confessions*, trans. Henry Chadwick (Oxford: Oxford University Press, 1991), p. 124 [Bk. VII, ch. 10, §16].

true community and relating to others according to laws of exchange (abstract labour); the gift is privatized. Property is commodified and thus made alienable. In contrast, as Jean-Luc Marion stresses, what is transubstantiated is not *ousia* understood as property, a substance available for possession; the Eucharist is enacted by the pure gift of God, requiring only that we be disposed to receive it anew.[88] Milbank provides a corrective to Marion in pointing out that a certain kind of exchange does take place in the divine gift. Although it is true that we can never make a return to God, 'since there is nothing extra to God that *could* return to him,'[89] in the economy of the divine gift we participate in the divine life, such that the poles of giver and recipient are enfolded into God. In a capitalist economy, gifts are only possible privately, where the recipient is rendered passive and the giver experiences giving as an alienation of property. In the divine economy of gift, in contrast, as in pre-capitalist economies, the gift is not alienated from the giver, but the giver is in the gift, goes with the gift. For this reason in pre-capitalist economies a return is expected, but this is never a mere contract, since the return is not pre-established, but comes in an unpredictable form at an unpredictable time, bearing the character of the counter-giver. In the divine economy, this type of giving is perfected as the dualism of giver and recipient is collapsed; Christ is the perfect return of God to God. In the Eucharist, we receive the gift of Christ not as mere passive recipients, but by being incorporated into the gift itself, the Body of Christ. As members of the Body, we then become nourishment for others – including those not

---

[88] Jean-Luc Marion, *God Without Being*, trans. Thomas A. Carlson (Chicago: University of Chicago Press, 1991), pp. 95–101, 161–82.

[89] John Milbank, 'Can a Gift be Given?: Prolegomena to a Future Trinitarian Metaphysic,' *Modern Theology* 11 (1995), p. 133.

part of the visible Body – in the unending trinitarian economy of gratuitous giving and joyful reception.[90] Property and *dominium* are thus reconfigured.

The Eucharist aims at the building of the Body of Christ which is not simply centripetal; we are united not just to God as to the centre but to one another. This is no liberal body, in which the centre seeks to maintain the independence of individuals from each other, nor a fascist body, which seeks to bind individuals to each other through the centre. Christ is indeed the Head of the Body, but the members do not relate to one another through the Head alone, for Christ Himself is found not only in the centre but at the margins of the Body, radically identified with the 'least of my brothers and sisters' (Matt. 25.31–46), with whom all the members suffer and rejoice together (1 Cor. 12.26). Christ is the centre of the Eucharistic community, but in the economy of the Body of Christ, gift, giver, and recipient are constantly assimilated one to another, such that Christ is what we receive, He who gives it, and 'the least' who receives the gift, and we are assimilated to Christ in all three terms. Whereas in the modern state the centre either vindicates the rights of property against the marginalized or takes direct concern for the welfare of the marginalized out of our hands, in Christ the dichotomy of centre and periphery is overcome.

The unity of the state body depends, as we have seen, on the subsumption of the local and particular under the universal. This movement is a simulacrum of true catholicity, in which the antithesis of local and universal is effaced. The Eucharist gathers the many into one (cf. 1 Cor. 10.16–17) as an anticipation of the eschatological unity of all in Christ, but the local is not therefore simply subordinated to the universal.

[90] Milbank, pp. 119–61. See also John Milbank, 'Socialism of the Gift, Socialism by Grace,' *New Blackfriars* 77/910 (December 1996), pp. 532–48.

Indeed it is the local community where the Eucharist is found. As John Zizioulas points out, it was therefore possible for the early Church to speak of 'catholic Churches' in the plural, and to identify the 'whole Church' with the local church. Each Eucharist performed in the local community makes present not part of Christ but the whole Christ, and the eschatological unity of all in Christ. For this same reason, however, there can be no mutual exclusion between local Eucharistic communities. From the early centuries this principle was represented by the necessity for two or three bishops from other communities to participate in the ordination of any bishop. The Eucharist made it necessary to see the whole Christ in each local community, which at the same time united the communities, not through a single external centre or structure superimposed on the local, but through the presence of the whole Christ in each.[91] The one Christ, then, is the centre of each Eucharistic community, yet the centre appears in many different places. Here we might apply Alan of Lille's comment about absolute Being to the Body of Christ: it is an 'intelligible sphere whose center is everywhere and whose circumference is nowhere.'[92]

The Eucharist transgresses national boundaries and redefines who our fellow-citizens are. Rousseau was right to note that communion among churches is a threat to the unity of the state. The eschatological breakdown of divisions between Jew and Greek – and all other natural and social

[91] John Zizioulas, 'Eucharist and Catholicity' in *Being as Communion: Studies in Personhood and the Church* (Crestwood, NY: St Vladimir's Seminary Press, 1985), pp. 143–69. Catholic and Orthodox ecclesiologies provide a valuable check to each other on this point. The papacy guards against a tendency to Caesaropapism, but the Pope must be seen as Bishop of Rome, *primus inter pares*.

[92] Alan of Lille, quoted by St Bonaventure in *The Soul's Journey into God*, trans. Ewart Cousins (New York: Paulist Press, 1978), p. 100 [ch. V, §8].

divisions – is preeminently made present in the Eucharistic feast. Patristic writers tended to emphasize the eschatological dimension of the Eucharist,[93] regarding it as a foretaste of the heavenly banquet in which 'people from east to west, from north and south, will come and sit down at the feast in the kingdom of God' (Luke 13.29). Thus St John Chrysostom, in his commentary on Hebrews, displays the early Church's conviction that at the Eucharist the heavenly banquet irrupts into earthly time: 'For when our Lord Jesus lies as a slain Victim, when the Spirit is present, when He Who sits at the right hand of the Father is here, when we have been made children by baptism and are fellow-citizens with those in heaven, when we have our fatherland in heaven and our city and citizenship, when we are only foreigners among earthly things, how can all this fail to be heavenly?'[94] This is a fundamental disfigurement of the imagination of citizenship in the territorial state. One's fellow-citizens are not all present Britons or Germans, but fellow members (and potential members) of the Body of Christ, past, present, and future.

The Eucharist is not simply a promise of future bliss outside of historical time. In the biblical and patristic witness we find the Eucharist as an earthly practice of peace and reconciliation. Paul reprimands the Corinthians for continuing divisions between rich and poor, and suggests that some of them are sick and dying *now* because they have partaken of the Eucharist without first reconciling these divisions (1 Cor. 11.17–32). Where peace is lacking, the Eucharist appears as an eschatological sign of judgement requiring that people

[93] For documentation of this connection, see Geoffrey Wainwright, *Eucharist and Eschatology* (New York: Oxford University Press, 1981).

[94] St John Chrysostom, *In Heb. Hom.*, XIV, 1, 2. The translation is from Dom Gregory Dix, *The Shape of the Liturgy* (London: Dacre Press, 1945), p. 252.

reconcile before a true Eucharist can take place. For this reason the Didache requires that any who has differences with another not participate in the Eucharist until the two parties have reconciled[95] (see also Matt. 5.23–26). From the earliest times Christians have exchanged a kiss of peace before the Eucharist as an indication that the Eucharist demands reconciliation. This practice is a sign of a peace that cannot be specified through the formal adjudication of contractual obligations, but can only be constructed in the direct encounter of human beings who consider themselves members of one another and of the Prince of Peace.

This brief display of a few central Eucharistic themes is not intended to idealize the actual practice of the Eucharist in our divided churches. Clearly Christians have to an alarming degree adopted the salvation *mythos* of the state as their own, and submitted to the state's practices of binding. We submit to these practices, even give our bodies up for war, in the hope that the peace and unity promised by the state will be delivered. What I have tried to show is that the state *mythos* and state *religio* are distortions of our true hope, and that the Christian tradition provides resources for resistance.

For the most part, Christians have accepted the integrating role of the state on the assumption that the state is a 'secular' and therefore neutral apparatus for the working out of conflict among different interests. To see the state as an alternative soteriology, and civil society as inseparable from the state, is to begin to notice the inherent conflict between state practices and the practices such as the Eucharist which Christians take for granted. True peace depends not on the subsumption of this conflict, but on a recovered sense of its urgency.

---

[95] *The Didache*, §14.

2

THE MYTH OF CIVIL SOCIETY AS
FREE SPACE

There have been a number of recent attempts, Catholic and Protestant, to diagnose and overcome the claustrophobia induced by the Church's confinement to the private sphere. Most take the form, predictably enough, of arguing for the public potential of religion and encouraging Christians to get off the sidelines and into the game. 'Civil society' is a key concept for this reconfiguration.[1] It names a space that, above all, is public without being political in the usual sense of direct involvement with the state. This distinction between state and society is seen by some Christian social ethicists as a breakthrough concept because it seems to allow the Church to avoid mere privatization on the one hand, and the Constantinian spectre of implication in state coercion on the

---

[1] There has been an explosion of literature in political theory and social ethics on 'civil society.' Among many examples see Andrew Arato, *Civil Society, Constitution and Legitimacy* (Lanham, MD: Rowman and Littlefield, 2000); Benjamin R. Barber, 'The Search for Civil Society,' *The New Democrat*, no. 7 (March/April), 1995; Benjamin R. Barber, *Strong Democracy: Participatory Politics for a New Age* (Berkeley: University of California Press, 1984); Harry Boyte, *Commonwealth: A Return to Citizen Politics* (New York: Free Press, 1989); Sara Evans and Harry Boyte, *Free Spaces: The Sources of Democratic Change in America* (New York: Harper & Row, 1986); Jurgen Habermas, *Between Facts and Norms: Contributions to a Discourse Theory of Law and Democracy*, trans. William Rehg (Cambridge, MA: MIT Press, 1996). For a history of the concept, see John Ehrenberg, *Civil Society: The Critical History of an Idea* (New York: New York University Press, 1999).

53

other. Chastened by its experience with rule, yet aware of the absence of a privatized Christianity from the biblical and traditional witness, the Church seeks to speak clearly in the public arena without carrying a big stick.

In this chapter I will sketch two ways (of many, I hasten to add) in which the concept of civil society is currently being used to carve out a space for Christians to be 'public,' and then make some suggestions of problems that arise from these models. The first way involves the theoretical appropriation of John Courtney Murray's work by authors who advocate a 'public theology.' The second is a practical application of Harry Boyte's work on civil society which is being appropriated in Catholic schools to advance the public mission of Christian education. The first way is more oriented toward public policy, the second toward grassroots activism. Despite differences, however, I will argue that, though both seek to create a space for the Church that is both 'public' and 'free,' neither succeed. In this chapter I will try to show that, unless 'public' is redefined, being public is a game at which the Church will inevitably lose, in part because the very distinction of public and private, as we have seen, is an instrument by which the state domesticates the Church. I will then suggest that the Church can only resist state discipline through the use of its own Eucharistic resources through which it becomes a body of a peculiar type, the Body of Christ.

I. MURRAY AND FRIENDS

In Catholic circles the father of public theology is John Courtney Murray, who put tremendous emphasis on a sharp distinction between state and society. According to Murray, this distinction originates in the medieval distinction between, on the one hand, the *imperium*, and on the other the *ecclesia*, by which he indicates the entire Christendom, or *christianitas*. This distinction mirrors the distinction between temporal and spiritual. Just as the *imperium* served a limited role in medieval Christendom, so the American constitutional order establishes limits on the state.[2] The state in Murray's thought is but one limited part of society, that part responsible for the maintenance of public order and political administration; it is not responsible for the entirety of the common good. The essence of the state is its coercive function, but this function is exercised in the name of public peace. The state mediates and reconciles all the conflicts among different individuals and groups in civil society. The first two articles of the First Amendment of the American constitution are therefore 'articles of peace'[3] which perform the state's role of subsumption of conflict by excluding religious difference from the political sphere. The importance of the distinction between state and civil society is to carve out free space beyond the direct grasp of the state. Murray puts it this way: 'In general, "society" signifies an area of freedom, personal and corporate, whereas "state" signifies the area in which public powers may legitimately apply their coercive powers. To deny the distinction is to espouse the notion of government as totalitarian.'[4]

For the sake of civil peace, religion is excluded from the state but allowed to flourish in the remaining public space

---

[2] John Courtney Murray, SJ, 'The Problem of Religious Freedom' in *Religious Liberty: Catholic Struggles with Pluralism*, ed. J. Leon Hooper, SJ (Louisville: Westminster/John Knox Press, 1993), p. 144. Murray does not appear to deal with the problem of transposing the homogeneous wholeness of the term 'society' from the complex of overlapping personal loyalties that constituted medieval Christendom.

[3] John Courtney Murray, SJ, 'Civil Unity and Religious Integrity: The Articles of Peace' in *We Hold These Truths: Catholic Reflections on the American Proposition* (Kansas City: Sheed and Ward, 1960), pp. 45–78.

[4] Murray, 'The Problem of Religious Freedom,' pp. 144–5.

defined by civil society. Here the various religious 'conspiracies,' as he called them, could meet on common ground
and debate public life in the language – not of theology,
which tends to divide one from the other conspiracies – but of
natural law, the language of cool, dry reason. Natural law,
Murray thought, has no theological presuppositions; rather it
provides for the possibility of reasoned discourse among
religions and even with that 'conspiracy' which does not
acknowledge God at all.[5] Underlying this reasoned discourse,
and in part proceeding from it, is a public philosophy or
public consensus.[6] This consensus is not the sum of public
opinion or self-interest, but is based on certain truths that
structure the political system of the United States; 'we hold
these truths' because they are true.[7] This consensus does not
eliminate conflict, but rather serves as an agreed basis upon
which conflicts are in theory resolved.

For my present purpose it is important to see that for
Murray this consensus manages to maintain the fences which
make his distinction of state and society work. In the first
place, society is free of coercion precisely because there are
commonly agreed rules for discourse which are built into the
American proposition and are part of American experience.
Reasoned discourse guarantees that public conversation will
take place on the basis of persuasion, and not coercion. In the
second place – and this is seldom noticed in Murray's thought
– this consensus also maintains a proper distinction between

<hr>

[5] Murray, 'The Origins and Authority of the Public Consensus' in *We
Hold These Truths*, pp. 109–23.

[6] Murray uses the terms synonymously, saying that 'public philosophy'
emphasizes objectivity of content, whereas 'consensus' emphasizes a
subjectivity of persuasion; Murray, 'Two Cases for the Public Consensus:
Fact or Need' in *We Hold These Truths*, p. 79.

[7] Murray, 'The Origins and Authority of the Public Consensus' in *We
Hold These Truths*, pp. 98–106.

civil society and economic activity. Murray acknowledges the power and omnipresence of economic forces from which neither state nor church, family nor individual is immune. However, it is precisely the idea of the 'public consensus' that saves us from the overweening power of corporations and economic forces. Murray adopts his exposition of the 'public consensus' from Adolf Berle, who attributes the relative freedom America enjoys from abuses of economic power to this consensus. '[T]he ultimate protection of individuals lies not in the play of economic forces in free markets, but in a set of value judgments so widely accepted and deeply held in the United States that public opinion can energize political action when needed to prevent power from violating these values.'[8] Through the public consensus, the state is mobilized in its coercive function to keep economic power in check, without the state thereby overstepping the boundaries of its own power. State, civil society, and work are all separable into semi-autonomous, though interrelated, spheres.

Contemporary interpreters of Murray's project have adopted his distinction of state and society as central. In Richard John Neuhaus' conception of democracy, for example, it is crucial that there be many different actors in the 'public square.'

> The state is one actor among others. Indispensable to this arrangement are the institutional actors, such as the institutions of religion, that make claims of ultimate or transcendent meaning. The several actors in the public square – government, corporations, education, communications, religion – are there to challenge, check, and compete with one another.[9]

---

[8] Adolf Berle, quoted in Murray, 'The Origins and Authority of the Public Consensus,' p. 101.
[9] Richard John Neuhaus, *The Naked Public Square: Religion and Democracy in America* (Grand Rapids, MI: Wm. B. Eerdmans, 1984), p. 84.

The churches, then, take their rightful place as public institutions without direct implication in wielding coercive state power, entanglements that have had disastrous consequences in Western history.[10] As the state maintains a monopoly on legitimate coercion, the Church will not hope to intervene directly in state affairs, lest the spectre of religious warfare once again show its cadaverous face. It is here, outside the state, that the Church goes public in the broader sense of its participation in the free public debate and the formation of the religious sensibilities of its members. 'The activity of the US Catholic bishops on nuclear weapons and abortion, for example, is often directed toward policies which are established by the state, but the bishops' involvement in these issues occurs in and through the channels a democratic society provides for public debate,' writes Richard McBrien. 'In such a society voluntary associations play a key role, providing a buffer between the state and the citizenry as well as a structured means of influencing public policy. In the US political system the church itself is a voluntary association.'[11]

In his *The Naked Public Square*, Neuhaus makes his case for the public nature of religion by defining religion as 'all the ways we think and act and interact with respect to what we believe is ultimately true and important.'[12] Politics is a function of culture, and at the heart of culture is religion. Neuhaus argues

[10] Neuhaus, pp. 116–17.

[11] Richard McBrien, *Caesar's Coin* (New York: Macmillan Publishing Company, 1987), p. 42.

[12] Neuhaus, p. 27. Public theologian Richard McBrien similarly defines religion as '*the whole complexus of attitudes, convictions, emotions, gestures, rituals, symbols, beliefs, and institutions by which persons come to terms with, and express, their personal and/or communal relationship with ultimate Reality (God and everything that pertains to God),*' *Caesar's Coin*, p. 11. For their definition of religion, Michael and Kenneth Himes quote McBrien; see Michael J. Himes and Kenneth R. Himes, OFM, *The Fullness of Faith: The Public Significance of Theology* (New York: Paulist Press, 1993), pp. 19–20.

that it would be foolish therefore to try to denude the public square of religion, for it is very much a part of what drives our life together. Law derives its legitimacy from the fact that it expresses 'what people believe to be their collective destiny or ultimate meaning.'[13] The state is, as Neuhaus says, 'not the source but the servant of the law,'[14] and the law derives from the deepest moral intuitions of the people. The law of the land is thus the embodiment of the network of binding obligations, the *religare*, from which is derived the word 'religion.'[15] Granted, Neuhaus admits, religion in the past has been banned for fear of the kind of fanaticism that tore apart Europe in the era of the religious wars, but he argues that today the only way to prevent politics from degenerating into a violent struggle for power is by constructing a public ethic built on the operative values of the American people, 'values that are overwhelmingly grounded in religious belief.'[16] Religion is not to be narrowly understood, however, for religion and culture are impossible to distinguish sharply; Neuhaus draws on Clifford Geertz to argue that religion is the 'ground or depth-level of culture'[17] and must therefore be present in building a common political culture based on peaceful consensus.

If consensus is the goal, however, Neuhaus claims that religion must gain access to the public sphere with arguments that are public in nature. The problem with the Moral Majority is that '*it wants to enter the political arena making public claims on the basis of private truths*,' that is, arguments 'derived from sources of revelation or disposition that are essentially private and arbitrary.'[18] As another Murrayite, George Weigel, says:

[13] Neuhaus, p. 256.
[14] Neuhaus, p. 259.
[15] Neuhaus, pp. 250–1.
[16] Neuhaus, p. 37.
[17] Neuhaus p. 132.
[18] Neuhaus, p. 36.

> Those who enter the civil public square have a right to
> speak from religious conviction. But those who claim a
> right to speak assume a responsibility to speak in such a
> way that they can be heard ... In concrete practice, this
> will mean 'translating' religiously-based moral claims
> and arguments into concepts and language that can be
> heard and contested by fellow-citizens of different
> faiths.[19]

This follows from Weigel's definition of 'public' as 'under-
standable to all.'[20]

Not all interpreters of Murray are content with Murray's
banishment of theological language from the public square.
Michael and Kenneth Himes, for example, in their book *The
Fullness of Faith*, have pleaded for the public significance of
theology, though under certain limited conditions. According to the Himeses, clarity about the distinction between
state and society ought not obscure the fact that there is
some interpenetration between the two. This recognition
likewise demands a recognition that people who act in the
realm of the state do so having been formed by religion.[21]
This formation takes place primarily in the hearts and minds
of believers who, though acting publicly, have been shaped
in their 'basic orienting attitudes' by explicitly religious
symbols. More than this, though, the Himeses wish to allow
the use of theological language in the public forum, even
though the listeners may not share the faith of the speaker.
Although public debate in civil society must be based on a
consensus among all people, religious or not, on what can be
considered reasonable, religious people should not shy away

[19] George Weigel, *Catholicism and the Renewal of American Democracy* (New
York: Paulist Press, 1989), p. 116.
[20] Neuhaus, p. 115.
[21] Himes and Himes, pp. 14–15.

from using religious symbols, such as the Trinity, in the hope that they may communicate something universal even to those who reject the theological origins of such symbols. Here the Himeses turn to David Tracy's concept of the 'classic,' defined as 'a phenomenon whose excess and permanence of meaning resists definitive interpretation.'[22] In the presence of such a classic in art or religion, for example, even the uninitiated is subject to the transmission of some truth which is therefore a public truth. The Himeses also adopt Tracy's suggestion that one concentrate on the 'effects' of such truth, and not its non-public 'origins' in the doctrine of one particular religion.[23]

Theology has thus an important contribution to make to the public life of a society. Nevertheless, when moving from civil society to state, the 'basic orienting attitudes' that theological symbols elicit must be translated into public policy by means of a social ethic, that is, theories of justice, the state, and so on, which cannot be derived directly from theology; 'public theology is several steps removed from public policy.'[24] The Trinity, for example, must first be translated into a concept of 'relationality' which belongs to social ethics, and then into an affirmation of a certain kind of rights-language.[25] The result in theory is a theology which is free to function in a fully public manner but yet not in a way that seeks to impose its alien beliefs on the other. The Church stands in a position to form hearts and minds, to equip them for public life, but the Church remains of course outside access to the coercive power of the

---

[22] David Tracy, quoted in Himes and Himes, p. 16.
[23] David Tracy, in Himes and Himes, p. 16.
[24] David Tracy, in Himes and Himes, pp. 22–3.
[25] David Tracy, in Himes and Himes, pp. 55–73.

state, and theology remains subject to the bar of what the society can consider 'reasonable.'[26]

[26] European 'political theology' first elaborated in the 1960s has many affinities with 'public theology' in its approach to state and civil society. Johann Baptist Metz, for example, also begins with the acceptance of the 'proper' emancipation of the political from the religious. The Enlightenment for Metz signifies the achievement of the maturity of human freedom. The secularized political order is an order of freedom; political realities are no longer given but are subject to free human action. Secularization is not the dethroning of Christ in the world, but rather 'the decisive point of his dominion in history,' for it is Christianity which sets the world free to be itself; Metz, *Theology of the World*, trans. William Glen-Doepel (New York: Seabury Press, 1969), p. 19. Crucial to this emancipation is the distinction between state and civil society, which has the effect of limiting the state's pretensions. Civil society is the central open forum of a given nation-state in which all groups freely participate. The Church now no longer seeks to dominate and establish a Christian state, but rather takes its place in civil society alongside other societal groupings. Here in civil society consensus is achieved on which public policies the state, which holds a monopoly on coercive power, should establish and enforce.

Metz' new version of political theology considers the old versions of Bonald, Donoso Cortés, Schmitt, and others – which believe that theology can politicize directly – to be 'precritical' because they do not accept the Enlightenment critique of religion. At the same time, however, Metz is concerned that the legitimate separation of the Church from the political sphere does not result in the mere privatization of the Christian faith, the delivering over of the Gospel to the anaemic embrace of bourgeois sentimentality. Metz' solution is that the Church take its place in civil society as an 'institution of social criticism' whose mission is defined as a service to the history of freedom unfolding since the Enlightenment. On the basis of the memory of Jesus' confrontation with the powers and his preference for the marginalized, the Church will criticize all social forms as falling short of the Kingdom of God. Even the Church itself is put under the ' "eschatological proviso," ' which makes every historically real status of society appear to be provisional.' The criticism the Church provides is not merely negative, but a challenge to make actual in the present the eschatological promises of the biblical tradition: freedom, peace, justice, and reconciliation. Because theology cannot be directly politicized, however, theology must be translated into 'practical public reason' for consumption in the arena of civil society; see Metz, pp. 107–14.

II. PUBLIC ACHIEVEMENT

The Murrayite models sketched so briefly here depend on the maintenance of a space in society outside the reach of the state, yet Murray and his successors share a tendency to see that space as oriented toward the state. Free discussion takes place outside of the state in civil society, yet such debate is oriented ultimately toward the making of public policy. Though theoretically limited, the state is still the primary means for the establishment of justice. This is the case whether what is primarily in mind are either lobbying efforts by the social justice arms of the Church bureaucracy aimed at producing legislation, or efforts aimed at affecting 'culture' as a whole. There is talk of 'the' (singular) public square. The 'common' to which the 'common good' refers is the nation-state. 'The health-care debate' has to do with legislation before Congress on government-sponsored health care insurance, prescription drug price controls, Medicare, and so on.

There is another model of civil society, however, which is beginning to have an increasing impact in Christian circles. It shares with the Murrayite models an emphasis on the creation and maintenance of free spaces in society outside the direct purview of the state. Unlike the Murrayite models, however, its accent is not on public policy but on the democratic potential of civil society itself. One important exemplification of this model is based on the work of Harry Boyte, one of the principal interlocutors in the debates over civil society. From the Humphrey Institute at the University of Minnesota, Boyte has been advocating the renewal of American democracy through the empowerment of grassroots citizens' groups. In addition to extensive publishing in the field, Boyte is also something of an activist. One of his more prominent endeavours is called 'Public Achievement,' an attempt to instil the virtues of citizenship into school-age children. Public Achievement has been very active in Catholic schools in my area, and the social justice office of the archdiocese has just begun a major collaboration with Boyte to use Public Achievement as a means of training Catholic school students in the public use of Catholic social teaching. At St Bernard's Catholic school, Public Achievement has taken root and changed the culture of the school. Every Thursday morning is given over to Public Achievement, facilitating involvement for every student in every grade. St Bernard's has been made a national model for the creation of a Catholic School of Democracy and Social Justice.[27]

For Boyte the term 'civil society' conveys three important themes in democratic theory, all derived from recent democratic movements in the US, the Third World, and especially Eastern Europe during the fall of communism.[28] The first is a renewed appreciation for the quotidian and mundane types of power wielded by ordinary citizens. There is a small movement to break the preponderant concentration of political science on electoral politics and parties to the exclusion of the actual decision-making taking place in concrete communities. Boyte has been structuring his work around case studies of community organizations.[29] The second is the importance of alternative sources of power as bulwarks against the state. It has long been a bias of left-wing

[27] Harry Boyte, Nancy Kari, Jim Lewis, Nan Skelton, and Jennifer O'Donoghue, *Creating the Commonwealth: Public Politics and the Philosophy of Public Work* (Dayton, OH: Kettering Foundation, n.d.), p. 18.

[28] Harry C. Boyte, 'Off the Playground of Civil Society,' *The Good Society* 9, no. 2 (1999), pp. 1, 4.

[29] Boyte's book *Citizen Action and the New American Populism*, co-authored with Heather Booth and Steve Max (Philadelphia: Temple University Press, 1986) consists almost entirely of such case studies. Boyte's *CommonWealth: A Return to Citizen Politics* (New York: Free Press, 1989) interweaves such case studies with a more general democratic theory.

politics especially to think big, to 'see like a state,' as the title of James Scott's recent book has it.[30] 'Civil society' became an energizing concept for the movements of 1989 that brought down totalitarian regimes from the inside. The third is an appreciation of the free and uncoerced nature of discourse in voluntary community settings. Boyte and Sara Evans have pioneered the study of what they call 'free spaces,' defined as 'settings between private lives and large-scale institutions where people can act with dignity, independence and vision. These are, in the main, voluntary forms of association with a relatively open and participatory character' which include many religious organizations, clubs, self-help groups, and so on.[31] The black Church is singled out as an autonomous institution that has, at various points in American history, allowed the very possibility of free speech that opposed the dominant culture. For Boyte, such institutions are not merely important for their own sake, but as seedbeds of democratic movements with much broader impact. The civil rights movement, begun in the black Church, is, for Boyte, a particularly important paradigm of 'democratic renewal.'[32]

Rather than fix on 'the' public debate as supervised by the state, therefore, Boyte wants to encourage democratic renewal as it springs from local community action. That said, however, Boyte is critical of those he calls 'voluntarists,' who would locate active citizenship in voluntary organiza-tions and leave it there. Can we seriously expect, Boyte

[30] See James Scott, *Seeing Like a State* (New Haven, CT: Yale University Press, 1998). Scott's earlier work includes a fascinating book called *Weapons of the Weak*, a study of poor people's ordinary ways of resistance to power, which typically involve foot-dragging, false compliance, sabotage, and the like, and not more dramatic revolutionary uprisings.

[31] Sara M. Evans and Harry C. Boyte, *Free Spaces: Sources of Democratic Change in America* (New York: Harper & Row, 1986), pp. 17–18.

[32] Evans and Boyte, pp. 26–68.

sharply asks, to confront power with 'volunteers'?[33] Here Boyte is critical of theorists such as Benjamin Barber who define 'civil society' (like Murray) over against both government and economic activity. For Barber, civil society is a kind of refuge from the coercion of the state and the consumerism of the market, a position that Boyte regards as fatalistic.[34] According to Boyte, democratic renewal must not remain confined to 'free spaces,' but must challenge institutions such as the state and the corporation. Crucial to this challenge is the idea of 'public work,' which Boyte and Nancy Kari define as 'patterns of work that have public dimensions (that is, work with public purposes, work by a public, work in public settings) as well as the "works" or products themselves.'[35] In blurring the lines between 'public' and 'work,' Boyte and Kari hope to renew a sense that America is not built in volunteers' spare time, but is the product of people's day to day labours. The workplace is reclaimed as a potentially public space, and what is usually considered public is recast as the work of ordinary citizens, not merely the operations of the distant state bureaucracy.

Boyte is also critical of those he calls 'moralists,' who blame the deterioration in democratic practice not on government or the economy but on declining morality and a lack of personal responsibility. While Boyte advocates a renewal of

[33] Boyte, 'Off the Playground of Civil Society,' pp. 4–5.

[34] Boyte, 'Off the Playground of Civil Society,' pp. 4–5. For Barber's position, see his *A Place for Us: How to Make Society Civil and Democracy Strong* (New York: Hill and Wang, 1998). Habermas likewise writes of the 'self-limitation of civil society' to those spheres outside of the economy and the state, since both state bureaucracies and markets are now too complex to be directed by democratic processes; see Habermas, *Between Facts and Norms*, pp. 366–73.

[35] Harry C. Boyte and Nancy N. Kari, *Building America: The Democratic Promise of Public Work* (Philadelphia: Temple University Press, 1996), p. 202.

citizens' sense of personal ownership for what is public, he believes it is wrong to blame the citizens for what has gone wrong in American democracy. Absent from the moralists' considerations, says Boyte, is a serious analysis of why Americans feel so powerless, and the overwhelming forces of government and market which produce passivity in people.[36] To practise civil society is unavoidably to speak in terms of power. Boyte would perhaps be critical at this point of the Murrayite emphasis on reason over power. Though Boyte himself accents consensus-building, such emerges in the rough-and-tumble of competing power, not in some arid forum of public reasonableness.

One place where theory meets practice in Boyte's work is in Public Achievement, now being used in Catholic schools. The stated goal is to educate young people 'to think and act as citizens;'[37] St Bernard's School has adopted the theme 'Educating Catholic Citizens for the 21st Century.'[38] The method is to engage them in 'public work,' here defined as 'the hard, ongoing effort of working with a diverse group of people to solve public problems and to make things of lasting contribution in shaping and creating our communities and the wider world.'[39] Guided by a coach, a team of young people decides on a problem to address, then takes action.

[36] Boyte, 'Off the Playground of Civil Society,' pp. 5–6. Boyte has in mind especially *A Call to Civil Society: Why Democracy Needs Moral Truths*, a statement put out in the summer of 1998 by the Council on Civil Society, chaired by Jean Bethke Elshtain. The statement had a wide range of signatories, from Cornel West to Republican Senator Dan Coats of Indiana.

[37] *Building Worlds, Transforming Lives, Making History: A Guide to Public Achievement*, 2nd ed. (Minneapolis: Center for Democracy and Citizenship, 1998), p. 1. This is the training manual for coaches and participants in Public Achievement.

[38] Boyte, *et al.*, *Creating the Commonwealth*, p. 23.

[39] *Building Worlds, Transforming Lives, Making History*, p. 1.

Examples of issues range from the need for a skateboarding park to racism in the community to US policy on endangered animals or undocumented workers.[40] Actions include appeals to responsible authorities, letter-writing, fundraising, community awareness projects, and other activities.

A theory of civil society is embedded in this practice, and Public Achievement is centred on inculcating this theory and developing 'public identities' in young people. Weekly debriefing sessions offer reflection on core Public Achievement concepts, such as 'co-creation of learning, public work, self-interest, and power.'[41] Democracy is defined as the 'work of the people,'[42] not merely the work of political professionals. Furthermore, democracy means 'more than a people's right to participate in governance, it means all people hold power and can exercise it to create our common world.'[43] Freedom is defined as the ability of individuals to 'choose their life and their ends unobstructed by others,' though it is acknowledged as possible that the collective self-determination of the society could override an individual's self-determination.[44]

This last point is significant. No particular ends are given, other than the renewal of American democracy. Much emphasis is put on dealing with a diversity of people who will have a diversity of ends. How issues are chosen therefore depends on the self-interest of participants: 'Traditional forms of civic education focus on institutional politics ... or community service (e.g., helping those in need). Public Achievement departs from these approaches by giving explicit

[40] The students and teachers of St Bernard's were cited by Governor Jesse Ventura in his 1999 State of the State address for their successful attempt to build a new playground.
[41] Boyte, et al., Creating the Commonwealth, p. 18.
[42] Building Worlds, Transforming Lives, Making History, p. 40.
[43] Building Worlds, Transforming Lives, Making History, p. 23.
[44] Building Worlds, Transforming Lives, Making History, p. 23.

attention to the self-interest of participants, and to concepts of public contribution in a world of diverse values and cultures'.[45] As this passage indicates, self-interest is not defined narrowly. One of Public Achievement's primary themes is moving away from a view of politics as based on what I/we can get from the government.[46] The Public Achievement participant is made aware that a range of interests exists from self-interest to a broader conception of the public interest. Nevertheless, the participant is alerted to the importance of interests, and informed that 'a basic premise of public work is that people are more likely to become active on an issue that they feel strongly about.'[47] With no ends given, Public Achievement must recognize that the self-interest of individuals and groups will play a key role in determining what problems are approached and how they are approached. Public interest, therefore, emerges from a process of consensus building by which it is hoped that agreement on ends can be reached among diverse people with diverse interests.[48] Consensus is by no means undergirded by a strong conception of truth, as it is for Murray.

[45] Boyte, *et al.*, *Creating the Commonwealth*, p. 14.

[46] *Building Worlds, Transforming Lives, Making History*, p. 39. Public Achievement is differentiated from the 'civics approach,' which stresses receiving goods and services from the government, and the 'communitarian approach,' which can become too narrowly focused on the interests and experience of one relatively homogeneous group. For Boyte's own criticism of interest-organizing, see his *CommonWealth*, pp. 12–13.

[47] *Building Worlds, Transforming Lives, Making History*, p. 23. Self-interest appears to be a legitimate starting point provided it results in public action. Thus Public Achievement at St Bernard's is described as 'a vehicle for students to act on their self-interest in public ways around work to make change'; Boyte, *et al.*, *Creating the Commonwealth*, p. 15.

[48] Boyte, *et al.*, *Creating the Commonwealth*, p. 16.

III. PROBLEMS

I am entirely in agreement with the attempt to envision a space for the Church that is neither Constantinian nor privatized. There is much to applaud in the Himeses' attempt to allow theology out of the ghetto of private discourse. Boyte's scheme goes further in breaking out of a narrow focus on the making of public policy. I am in deep sympathy with Boyte's populism, his appreciation for the churches as potential 'free spaces' which escape the hegemony of the state. Christian educators' attempts to use Boyte's ideas in the form of Public Achievement have the potential to aid in moving the churches' political discourse and activism beyond limp recommendations on how to vote. Nevertheless, I want to point to some problems that undercut these attempts to give the Church a significant public presence.

To begin, both the Murrayites and Boyte are far too reticent about the interpenetration of state and society. In both models civil society appears as an essentially free space outside the coercive reach of the state. The flows of power tend to move from civil society to the state, such that the ultimate goal of democratic organization and social movement – even for Boyte – is to generalize the impact of such movements through influencing the state. The potential of every person to limit, control, and use the state is highlighted in a fashion not too distinct from the 'civics' approach that Boyte criticizes. Though Boyte's approach emphasizes power more than the Murrayite stress on reasoned consensus, power nevertheless tends to be envisioned as flowing in one direction, from civil society to state.

Insofar as they are speaking descriptively, however, I find this view of civil society far from convincing. As political scientist Michael Budde has written, 'Murray's theory of the state, such as it is, can only be described as naive, almost a direct transferral from civics texts to political description.'[49] In a society in which up to a third of the work force labours directly or indirectly for the state, it is simply empirically false to claim that the state is a small and limited part of the wider societal whole, regardless of the intentions of the Founding Fathers. In fact the supposedly free debate of the public square is disproportionately affected by the state. What counts as news is increasingly determined by spin doctors and media handlers. The media looks for its sources among government spokespersons and various 'experts' closely linked with the state apparatus.

Beyond the issue of 'big government,' however, other political scientists writing on the state in late capitalism tend to emphasize the extent to which civil society and the state have been fused into different moments of a single complex.[50] The economic, political, social and cultural spheres have merged to such an extent that culture obeys the logic of the market and the political apparatuses in turn create spaces for capital to operate. What is permissible as public discourse increasingly obeys the logic of accumulation; state-funded school lunch programmes are defended in terms of increasing students' performance and thus enhancing the country's position in the global economy vis-à-vis the Japanese.[51] In this way the state-society complex comes to disempower and co-opt other forms of discourse, such as that of the Church.

[49] Michael L. Budde, *The Two Churches: Catholicism & Capitalism in the World System* (Durham, NC: Duke University Press, 1992), p. 115.

[50] See, for example, Michael Hardt, 'The Withering of Civil Society,' *Social Text* 45, vol. 14, no. 4 (Winter 1995); Bob Jessop, *State Theory* (University Park, PA: The Pennsylvania State University Press, 1990), pp. 338–69; Antonio Negri, *The Politics of Subversion*, trans. James Newell (Cambridge: Polity Press, 1989), pp. 169–99; and Kenneth Surin, 'Marxism(s) and "The Withering Away of the State," ' *Social Text* no. 27 (1990), pp. 42–6.

[51] I owe this example to Professor Romand Coles of Duke University.

Imagining that the state is a limited part of society only makes the Church more vulnerable to its own debilitation. The state is not simply a mechanism for the representation of the freely gathered general will, nor is it a neutral instrument at the disposal of the various classes. It is rather, in the words of Kenneth Surin, an institutional assemblage which has as its task 'the modification and neutralization, primarily by its symbolic representations of social classes, of the efforts of resistance on the part of social subjects.' The state, as Surin puts it, 'subserves the processes of accumulation by representing the whole world of social production for its subjects as something that is "natural," as an inevitability.'[52] Thus, for example, the 'laws' of supply and demand and maximization of self-interest are presented as responding to human nature, and economists' predictions are held to be descriptive of reality rather than prescriptive, when they are in fact both.

The history of the modern state shows that it is not simply the instrument of the will of the people expressed through the organs of civil society. In fact the modern sovereign state has been *defined* by its usurping of power from lesser communal bodies. The view that the state is a natural outgrowth of family and community is extremely questionable. As Robert Nisbet points out, the modern state arose from *opposition* to kinship and other local social groupings; '[t]he history of the Western State has been characterized by the gradual absorption of powers and responsibilities formerly resident in other associations and by an increasing directness of relation between the sovereign authority of the State and the individual citizen.'[53]

Examples of this process are innumerable: the intervention

---

[52] Surin, p. 45.
[53] Robert A. Nisbet, *The Quest for Community* (London: Oxford University Press, 1953), p. 104.

of the state in matters of kinship, property, and inheritance; the conception of the law as something 'made' or legislated by the state rather than 'disclosed' from its divine source through the workings of custom and tradition; the abolition of ecclesiastical courts and the transfer of sole judicial proprietorship to the crown; the replacement of local duties and privileges by the rights of interchangeable individuals; the enclosure of common lands; the state's securing of a monopoly over legitimate violence.[54] Undergirding these and countless other instances is the use of Roman law on the Continent to arrogate to the state the sole privilege of recognizing the existence of lesser associations; such associations become endowed with a purely 'fictitious' personality, a *nomen juris* given from the centre by royal fiat rather than developed organically.[55]

State sovereignty and the debilitation of other associations were not meant to oppress but rather to free the individual; even more state-centred theorists such as Hobbes and Rousseau are quite clear on this point. As Nisbet makes plain, 'The real conflict in modern political history has not been, as is so often stated, between State and individual, but between State and social group.'[56] Indeed, the rise of the state is predicated on the creation of the individual. The

---

[54] Nisbet, pp. 102–8.

[55] On this development see John Neville Figgis, 'Churches in the Modern State' in *The Pluralist Theory of the State: Selected Writings of G. D. H. Cole, J. N. Figgis, and H. J. Laski*, ed. Paul Q. Hirst (London: Routledge, 1989), pp. 111–27. Figgis points out that, although Roman law as such was never adopted in England, an equivalent doctrine of state recognition of associations developed as part of the general trend toward centralization in the sixteenth century and after; ibid., p. 114. Ironically this nominalist doctrine, which would be used to reduce the Church to a purely 'voluntary association,' was first borrowed from Roman law by Pope Innocent IV; see Nisbet, p. 113.

[56] Nisbet, p. 109.

realization of a single, unquestioned political centre would make equivalent and equal each individual before the law, thereby freeing the individual from the caprice of local custom and subloyalties which would divide them from their fellow-citizens. For example, the dissolution of the medieval guild system and the endless 'interventions' of religious custom in economic matters is what unleashes the 'free' market.[57] The power of the state grew in concert with the rise of capitalism, because of direct state subsidies for business and international trade, the development of state-sanctioned standardized monetary and taxation systems, and the emergence of a centralized legal system which made possible the commodification and contractualization of land, goods, and especially labour. In other words, the impersonal and centralized state accompanied the invention of the autonomous individual liberated from the confines of the traditional group and now relating to other individuals on the basis of contract. Property – including one's own self in the form of one's labour – became *alienable*. Thus was born both the capitalist and the wage labourer.[58]

In an article entitled 'War Making and State Making as Organized Crime,' sociologist Charles Tilly explores the analogy of the state's monopoly on legitimate violence with the protection rackets run by the friendly neighbourhood mobster. According to Tilly 'a portrait of war makers and state makers as coercive and self-seeking entrepreneurs bears a far greater resemblance to the facts than do its chief

---

[57] See, for example, Adam Smith, *The Wealth of Nations* (New York: The Modern Library, 1937), pp. 740–65, 775–7 [Bk V, ch. 1, Part III, Art. III]. Smith details how the rise of commerce was accompanied by the dissolution of 'the ties of interest' which bound the classes to one another, as facilitated by the Church.

[58] Anthony Giddens, *The Nation-State and Violence* (Berkeley: University of California Press, 1987), pp. 148–71.

alternatives: the idea of a social contract, the idea of an open market in which operators of armies and states offer services to willing customers, the idea of a society whose shared norms and expectations call forth a certain kind of government.'[59] States extort large sums of money and the right to send their citizens out to kill and die in exchange for protection from violence both internal and external to the state's borders. What converts state war making from 'protection' to 'protection racket' is the fact that often states offer defence from threats which they themselves create, threats which can be imaginary or the real results of the state's own activities. Furthermore, the internal repression and the extraction of money and bodies for 'defence' that the state carries out are frequently among the most substantial impediments to the ordinary citizens' livelihood. The 'offer you can't refuse' is usually the most costly. The main difference between Uncle Sam and the Godfather is that the latter did not enjoy the peace of mind afforded by official government sanction.[60]

Building on Arthur Stinchcombe's work on legitimacy, Tilly shows that historically what distinguished 'legitimate' from 'illegitimate' violence had little to do with the assent of the governed or the religious sentiments which bind us. The distinction was secured by states' effective monopolization of the means of violence within a defined territory, a gradual process only completed in Europe with the birth of the modern state in the sixteenth and seventeenth centuries. The line between state violence and banditry was a fluid one early in the state-making process. Eventually the personnel of states

[59] Charles Tilly, 'War Making and State Making as Organized Crime,' in *Bringing the State Back In*, eds. Peter B. Evans, Dietrich Rueschemeyer, Theda Skocpol (Cambridge: Cambridge University Press, 1985), p. 169.

[60] Tilly, pp. 170–1.

were able to purvey violence more efficiently and on a wider scale than the personnel of other organizations.[61]

The process of making states was inseparable from the pursuit of war by the power elites of emergent states. As Tilly tells it, 'the people who controlled European states and states in the making warred in order to check or overcome their competitors and thus to enjoy the advantages of power within a secure or expanding territory.'[62] To make more effective war, they attempted to secure regularized access to the money and the bodies of their subjects. Building up their war-making capacity, and the birth of standing armies, increased in turn their power to eliminate rivals and monopolize the extraction of these resources from subject populations. These activities of extraction were facilitated by the rise of tax-collection apparatuses, courts, and supporting bureaucracies, in short, the rise of the modern state capable of realizing administrative sovereignty over a defined territory.[63]

The assent of the governed *followed*, and is to a large extent *produced by*, state monopoly on the means of violence within its borders. As a general rule, people are more likely to ratify the decisions of an authority that controls substantial force, both from fear of retaliation and, for those who benefit from stability, the desire to maintain that stability.[64] As Tilly puts it, 'A tendency to monopolize the means of violence makes a government's claim to provide protection, in either the comforting or the ominous sense of the word, more credible and more difficult to resist.'[65]

In contrast to the Murrayite model, in which power flows from civil society to state, other political theorists beginning

[61] Tilly, pp. 170–5.
[62] Tilly, p. 172.
[63] Tilly, pp. 172–86.
[64] Tilly, pp. 171–5.
[65] Tilly, p. 172.

with Hegel have drawn the flows of power in the opposite direction, from state to civil society. For Hegel, the associations of civil society take on an educative function between the state and the individual. Work is not excluded from Hegel's definition of civil society. Rather, civil society is where concrete labour is converted to abstract labour, that is, where the raw, untamed forces of labour are taken up by the institutions of civil society – such as trade unions, schools, and corporations – and domesticated for the sake of the universal interest of society. Labour, and all the interests and ends of individuals, must pass through the educative project of civil society before they can be fully realized, gathered, and universalized in the state, which is the 'actuality of the ethical Idea.'[66] Though based on production and family, the state is not the result of them, but rather comes first and is the true ground of them according to Hegel.[67] Work, family, and the person herself only becomes 'real,' takes on objectivity, by participation in the state.

Michel Foucault has shown in empirical detail how what Hegel considered the ideal has become a baleful reality. The institutions of civil society – the party, the union, the school, the corporation, the Church, the prison – have an educative or disciplinary function which realizes the state project.[68] Rather than seeing the labour union, for example, as the representative of the interests of workers in the open debate for influencing state policy, Foucault describes the way that unions serve to mediate the antagonisms of capitalist social relations and produce workers who are supportive of the capitalist state. The hyperpatriotism of unions (and churches)

[66] G. W. F. Hegel, *The Philosophy of Right*, trans. T. M. Knox (Oxford: Clarendon Press, 1952), §257.

[67] Hegel, §256.

[68] See for example Michel Foucault, *Discipline and Punish: The Birth of the Prison*, trans. Alan Sheridan (New York: Vintage Books, 1977), pp. 293–308.

during wartime illustrates this. It is not necessarily that the state directs a conscious conspiracy aimed at educating and propagandizing its citizens.[69] Surveillance has become a general feature of Western society, a feature that is one with state hegemony but does not depend on a totalitarian centre to enforce its rule. The power of Foucault's Panopticon image is precisely that *self*-discipline becomes the norm, reinforced by the pedagogical function of the apparently free institutions of civil society. As Michael Hardt argues in an essay entitled 'The Withering of Civil Society,' it is perhaps most descriptively accurate to say that there is no longer any significant distinction to be made between civil society and state, the two having been fused to such a great extent.[70] For example, government regulation – much of it for good ends – reaches into every facet of society and every type of activity. Furthermore, government is increasingly seen as a bureaucratic provider of goods and services whose primary job is to serve its 'customers,' a fact which Boyte himself laments. In arguing against the voluntarists, Boyte acknowledges the extent to which spaces in state, business, and civil society have come to resemble each other because they have been colonized by the rationalization of the market. He singles out the managerial culture of the mega-church, with its emphasis on attracting new congregants by providing them with specialized service, as a particularly bleak example.[71]

[69] See, for example, Michel Foucault, 'La gouvernementalité' in *Dits et écrits*, vol. 3 (Paris: Gallimard, 1994).

[70] Hardt, pp. 27–44.

[71] Boyte, 'Off the Playground of Civil Society,' p. 5. Examples of the interpenetration of state and society can be multiplied. One that comes immediately to mind is the official encouragement given to corporate mergers by government 'regulators.' What debate there is over such mergers is conducted around the question, 'Will this particular merger be good or bad for consumers?' People are defined as consumers, not citizens, by state management of the debate.

Today's gods do not respect the neat divisions between state, civil society, and economy, a point made sharply by Michel de Certeau:

> Seized from the moment of awakening by the radio (the voice is the law), the listener walks all day through a forest of narrativities, journalistic, advertising and televised, which, at night, slip a few final messages under the door of sleep. More than the God recounted to us by the theologians of the past, these tales have a function of providence and predestination: they organize our work, our celebrations – even our dreams – in advance. Social life multiplies the gestures and modes of behaviour *imprinted* by the narrative models: it continually reproduces and stores up the 'copies' of narratives.[72]

If this interpenetration of state, society, and economy is indeed the case, then appeals to the idea of free space outside the state may not be sufficient for the creation of true alternative spaces. Indeed, a project like Public Achievement can be seen as fulfilling the kind of educative or disciplinary role that Hegel and Foucault envision for the institutions of civil society. Embedded in Public Achievement's definition of freedom, for instance, is an anthropology that allows assimilation to a democratic capitalist order but is not so easily assimilable to a Christian anthropology in which a person's ends are not chosen but given by God. If Christian children's 'public identities' are being formed to be citizens of the nation-state, those same students can perhaps be forgiven for forgetting that by baptism their 'citizenship is in heaven,' as Paul tells the Philippians (3.20), and that their fellow

---

[72] Michel de Certeau, 'Believing and Making People Believe' in Graham Ward, ed., *The Certeau Reader* (Oxford: Blackwell Publishers, 2000), p. 125.

citizens are the saints, as the Ephesians are reminded (2.19). In other words, it is difficult to conceive of the church as a 'free space' when we have been self-disciplined to avoid public Christian language even within our own schools.

In both the Murrayite and the Boyte models, the price to the Church of admission to the 'public' is a submission of its particular truth claims to the bar of public reason, a self-discipline of Christian speech. In the case of Public Achievement, particular Christian ends – such as an especial care for the poor before considerations of self-interest – are subjugated to a purely procedural search for consensus among a diversity of ends, none of which can ultimately claim a larger warrant than what issues from self-interested choice. Political theorist Romand Coles criticizes Boyte's pragmatism for its propensity – contrary to Boyte's intentions – to silence minority positions and unpopular claims to some measure of truth. An emphasis on drawing together many diverse voices can foster a need to converge *prematurely* around common goals. Coles argues that proposals to change the terms of political discourse that seem 'absurd' or 'divisive' to the mainstream are in danger of being silenced. 'Pragmatic politics can foster poor listening and a restless intolerance toward those who speak from angles and in idioms that are foreign to many in the organization or those in the middle to whom an organization would appeal.'[73] Thus although Boyte holds up the black Church as a model of a 'free space,' it is not clear how he could accommodate as public the outrageous truth claims some black churches might want to make, claims

---

[73] Romand Coles, 'Toward an Uncommon Commonwealth: Reflections on Boyte's Critique of Civil Society,' *The Good Society* 9, no. 2 (1999), p. 26. As examples of prematurely silenced forms of discourse, Coles cites 'supporting non-anthropocentric ecological ethics, animal rights, radical bending of gender roles, challenges to mainstream political, economic, and cultural practices from the vantage point of small minority positions.'

such as 'Jesus is Lord, and not just for us.' An even deeper problem, however, is the fact that Public Achievement, despite its claims, does present as given one ultimate end: the renewal of American democracy. On this point there is no talk of a diversity of ends; the achievement of American democracy is simply presented as the telos of one's actions and the proper object of one's faith.

Murray is at least clear that the public consensus is built not upon self-interest but upon God-given truth. Nevertheless, the Murrayite project represents the self-disciplining of the Church's ability to make theological claims in public. Theology must submit to what 'the public' can consider reasonable, where 'the public' is understood in terms of the nation-state. Christian symbols must be run through the sausage-grinder of social ethics before coming out on the other end as publicly digestible policy. As Talal Asad has shown, however, religion as a symbol system theoretically detachable from communities of discipleship is a modern invention that facilitated the absorption of the Church into the modern secular state. For the Himeses, ritual and symbol are generically distinct from instrumental or pragmatic actions. Christian symbols stand at one remove from the reality they represent, and they function (as Clifford Geertz maintains) to elicit motivations which are then translatable into publicly available actions. Christian symbols can elicit transformations apart from participation in a community of discipleship. However, as Asad points out in his study of medieval – especially Benedictine – practices, ritual was never imagined as a distinct activity separate from a complete programme of Christian discipline and discipleship. Indeed, religious symbols are never separable from bodily practices of discipline and power. In the modern era, Asad points out, '[d]iscipline (intellectual and social) would abandon religious space, letting "belief," "conscience," and "sensibility" take its place.'[74] This does not mean, however, that discipline has disappeared, only that it is now administered by the state, which is assumed to possess an absolute monopoly on the means of coercion. In the modern West the primary locus of discipline has become the state-society complex, and the Church has been essentially transformed into a semi-private voluntary association.[75]

A major problem with the attempt to make religion public is that it is still 'religion.' Asad shows how the attempt to identify a distinctive essence of religion, and thus protect it from charges that it is nothing more than an epiphenomenon of 'politics' or 'economics,' is in fact linked with the modern removal of religion from the spheres of reason and power.[76] Religion is a universal essence detachable from particular ecclesial practices, and as such can provide the motivation necessary for all citizens of whatever creed to regard the nation-state as their primary community, and thus produce peaceful consensus. As we have seen, religion as a trans-historical phenomenon separate from 'politics' is a creation of Western modernity designed to tame the Church. Religion may take different cultural and symbolic expressions, but it remains a universal essence generically distinct from political power which then must be translated into publicly acceptable 'values' in order to become public currency. Religion is detached from its specific locus in disciplined ecclesial practices so that it may be compatible with the modern Christian's subjection to the discipline of the state. Echoes of Bodin resound in the public theologians' attempt to make religion the glue that holds the commonwealth together.

---

[74] Talal Asad, *Genealogies of Religion: Discipline and Reasons of Power in Christianity and Islam* (Baltimore: Johns Hopkins University Press, 1993), p. 39.

[75] Asad, pp. 27–54.

[76] Asad, pp. 27–9.

Religion, that is, and not the Church, for the Church must be separated entirely from the domain of power.

The great irony, then, is that in trying to arrange for the Church to influence 'the public,' rather than simply *be* public, the public has reduced the Church to its own terms. Citizenship has displaced discipleship as the Church's public key. In banishing theology from the public sphere, the Church has found it difficult to speak with theological integrity even within the Church. The flows of power from Church to public are reversed, threatening to flood the Church itself.

It is little wonder many people find liturgy, sacrament, and doctrine to be irrelevant to the 'real world' of social problems. Christian symbol floats free from the Church, which theologically is a social reality in its own right. Christian symbol must be translated and replaced in order to escape ghettoization. In the Christian tradition, by contrast, the liturgy is more than a generator of symbols for individual consumption. It is, as the original Greek *leitourgia* suggests – and despite Public Achievement – the true 'work of the people,' the *ergon* of the *laos*. The Church gathered around the altar does not simply disperse and be absorbed into civil society when God's blessing sends it forth. The liturgy does more than generate interior motivations to be better citizens. The liturgy generates a body, the Body of Christ – the Eucharist makes the Church, in Henri de Lubac's words – which is itself a *sui generis* social body, a public presence irreducible to a voluntary association of civil society.

As this suggests, I think the deepest problem with the two models of civil society we have been examining is their anaemic ecclesiology. Their search for a public Christian presence that is neither private nor in the thrall of the state simply bypasses the possibility of the Church as a significant social space. Missing is even a basic Augustinian sense that the Church is itself an alternative 'space' or set of practices whose citizenship is in some sort of tension with citizenship in the *civitas terrena*. For Augustine not the *imperium* but the Church is the true *res publica*, the 'public thing;' the *imperium* has forfeited any such claim to be truly public by its refusal to do justice, by refusing to give God his due.[77] For the Murrayite and Boyte models, on the other hand, what is public is that space bounded by the nation-state. To enter the public is to leave behind the Church as a body. Individual Christians, fortified by 'basic orienting attitudes,' can enter public space, but the Church itself drops out of the picture. The Church is an essentially asocial entity that provides only 'motivations' and 'values' for public action. Christians must therefore find their politics and their publicness elsewhere, borrowing from the available options presented by the secular nation-state. If we wish to go public, we must take on the language of citizenship. When Catholic schoolchildren embrace the plight of undocumented workers they are told they are being 'citizens,' unaware that the very fact that these workers are denied citizenship is the cause of their plight.

IV. THE CHURCH AS PUBLIC SPACE

In the modern age, Christians have tended to succumb to the power of state soteriology, and they have often done so on Christian grounds. It is not enough to see what is called 'secularization' as the progressive stripping away of the sacred from some profane remainder. What we have instead is the substitution of one *mythos* of salvation for another; what's more, the successor *mythos* has triumphed to a great extent

---

[77] St Augustine of Hippo, *The City of God*, trans. Marcus Dods (New York: The Modern Library, 1950), XIX, §21–2.

because it mimics its predecessor.[78] In the dissociation of the Church from the sword, many Christians have seen the God of peace emancipated from captivity to the principalities and powers, and in national unity despite religious pluralism many have glimpsed the promise of the original Christian quest for unity and peace.

If the Church accedes to the role of a voluntary association of private citizens, however, it will lack the disciplinary resources to resist the State's *religare*, its practices of binding. The call for the Church to be 'public' is not, however, a call for the Church to take up the sword once again. In fact, it is precisely the opposite. I have contrasted Church discipline with state discipline in order to counter violence on behalf of the state, which has spilt so much blood in our time. Contesting the state's monopoly on violence does not mean that the Church should again get a piece of the action, yet another form of Constantinianism. What I have tried to argue is that the separation of the Church from power did nothing to staunch the flow of blood on the West's troubled pilgrimage. The pitch of war has grown more shrill, and the recreation of the Church as a voluntary association of practitioners of religion has only sapped our ability to resist. The discipline of the state will not be hindered by the Church's participation and complicity in the 'public debate.'

What would it mean to construe the Church as a public space in its own right? First we must be more precise about what 'public' means. In one sense I have been using the term negatively to mean 'not private,' that is, not confined to the individual or the home. It would be a mistake, however, simply to accept the dichotomy of public and private as it is currently construed. In the Christian tradition, the home is

---

[78] I am indebted here to John Milbank's argument which frames his *Theology and Social Theory*; see especially pp. 9–12.

not simply private space, simply *oikos*, in part because the home is always open to the community through the practice of hospitality (Luke 10.3–11), but also because the Church itself is a new 'family' that breaks down the isolation of the old family unit (Mark 3.20–35). As John Paul II says in his 'Letter to Families,' the family through the Church opens up to a wider 'public' space, the widest imaginable; the family is the 'fundamental "cell" of society' whose task is to extend its own 'communion of persons' to the creation of a 'civilization of love.' John Paul reminds us that etymologically the word 'civilization' is derived from *civis*, or citizen, but this meaning should not be confined to what is ordinarily construed as the civic or political; 'the most profound meaning of the term "civilization" is not merely political, but rather pertains to human culture.'[79]

The Church appears then as a reality that is neither *polis* nor *oikos*. Ephesians 2.19 uses both 'public' and 'private' language simultaneously: 'you are citizens (*sympolitai*) with the saints and also members of the household (*oikeioi*) of God.'[80] The early Christians borrowed the term *ekklesia* or 'assembly' from the Greek city-state, where *ekklesia* meant the assembly of all those with citizen rights in a given city. The early Christians thus refused the available language of guild or association (e.g. *koinon*, *collegium*) and asserted that the Church was not gathered around particular interests, but was interested in all things; it was an assembly of the whole. And yet the whole was not the city-state or empire, but the people of God. As Gerhard Lohfink points out, the ultimate source for the language of *ekklesia* is not the Greek city-state but the assembly of Israel at Sinai. In Deuteronomy the foundational

---

[79] Pope John Paul II, 'Letter to Families,' p. 13.

[80] See Reinhard Hütter, 'The Church as "Public": Dogma, Practice, and the Holy Spirit,' *Pro Ecclesia* 3, no. 3 (Summer 1994), pp. 334–61.

assembly of Israel at Mt Sinai takes place according to the formulaic phrase 'the day of the assembly.'[81] In using the term *ekklesia* the Church understood itself as the eschatological gathering of Israel. In this gathering those who are by definition excluded from being citizens of the *polis* and consigned to the *oikos* – women, children, slaves – are given full membership through baptism.

The gathering of Israel is made possible by certain detailed practices, structured by the Torah, and oriented toward the exclusive worship of God. What makes these practices 'public' is that no aspect of life is excluded from them. The Law makes clear that what one does with one's money, one's body, one's neighbour, even one's faeces are all within the ambit of the people's worship of God, and all these practices combined form a distinctive body of people. When I use the term 'discipline,' it refers to a performance of the body. According to Hugh of St Victor, 'it is discipline imposed on the body which forms virtue. Body and spirit are but one: disordered movements of the former betray outwardly (*foris*) the disarranged interior (*intus*) of the soul. But inversely, "discipline" can act on the soul through the body – in ways of dressing (*in habitu*), in posture and movement (*in gestu*), in speech (*in locutione*), and in table manners (*in mensa*).'[82] There is no disjunction between outer behaviour and inner religious piety. The modern construction of religion interiorizes it, and makes religion only a motivating force on bodily political and economic practices. The modern Church thus splits the body from the soul and purchases freedom of religion by handing the body over to the state.

[81] Gerhard Lohfink, *Does God Need the Church?: Toward a Theology of the People of God*, trans. Linda M. Maloney (Collegeville, MN: Liturgical Press, 1999), pp. 218–20.

[82] J. C. Schmitt, 'Le geste, la cathédrale et le roi,' quoted in Asad, p. 138.

The recovery of the Thomist idea of religion as a virtue is crucial to the Church's resistance to state discipline. The virtues involve the whole person, body and soul, in practices which form the Christian to the service of God. Furthermore the virtues are acquired communally, within the 'public' practices of an ecclesial community which, as the Body of Christ, witnesses to the ability to discern vice from virtue, or violence from peace. Christian 'political ethics,' therefore, is inseparable from an account of how virtues such as religion and peaceableness are produced and reproduced – or deformed – in the habitual practices of the Church. A public Christian presence cannot be the pursuit of influence over the powers, but rather a question of what kind of community disciplines we need to produce people of peace capable of speaking truth to power.

The virtues are acquired by disciplined following of virtuous exemplars. Discipline is therefore perhaps best understood as *discipleship*; whereas the discipline of the state seeks to create disciples of Leviathan, the discipline of the Church seeks to form disciples of Jesus Christ, the Prince of Peace. For this reason our discipline will more resemble martyrdom than military victory. Oscar Romero, the day before he was martyred, used his authority to *order* Salvadoran troops to disobey orders to kill.[83] Romero

[83] Archbishop Oscar Romero, 'The Church: Defender of Human Dignity' in *A Martyr's Message of Hope* (Kansas City: Celebration Books, 1981), p. 161. The relevant part of his sermon on March 23, 1980 reads as follows: 'I would like to issue a special entreaty to the members of the army, and specifically to the ranks of the National Guard, the police and the military. Brothers and sisters, you are our own people; you kill your own fellow peasants. Someone's order to kill should not prevail; rather, what ought to prevail is the law of God that says, "Do not kill." No soldier is obliged to obey an order against the law of God; no one has to fulfill an immoral law ... Why, in the name of God, and in the name of this suffering people whose cries rise up to the heavens every day in greater tumult, I

understood that the discipline of Christian discipleship was in fundamental tension with that of the army. He put it this way: 'Let it be quite clear that if we are being asked to collaborate with a pseudo peace, a false order, based on repression and fear, we must recall that the only order and the only peace that God wants is one based on truth and justice. Before these alternatives, our choice is clear: We will follow God's order, not men's.'[84]

What I am pointing to is not the discipline of coercion but its antidote, to be found in all those practices of the Christian Church which bind us to one another in the peace of Christ. Recall that Hobbes' two crucial moves in domesticating the Church were to make individuals adhere to the sovereign instead of to one another, and to deny the international character of the Church. In contrast, as some Latin American churches have shown us, the Christian way to resist institutionalized violence is to adhere to one another as Church, to act as a disciplined Body in witness to the world. As Romero wrote, 'The church is well aware that anything it can contribute to the process of liberation in this country will have originality and effectiveness only when the church is truly identified as church.'[85] The ecclesial base communities in Latin America come together as Church to incarnate disciplined communities of peace and justice without waiting for an illusory influence on the state while the poor go

cont.
implore them, I beg them, I order them, in the name of God: Cease the repression!'

[84] Archbishop Oscar Romero, homily, July 1, 1979, quoted in *The Church is all of You: Thoughts of Archbishop Oscar Romero*, trans. and ed. James R. Brockman, SJ (Minneapolis: Winston Press, 1984), p. 88.

[85] Archbishop Oscar Romero, 'The Church's Mission amid the National Crisis' in *Voice of the Voiceless*, trans. Michael J. Walsh (Maryknoll, NY: Orbis Books, 1985), p. 128.

hungry.[86] And the very Eucharistic practices by which the world is fed in turn join people into one Body which transcends the limits of the nation-state. To recognize Christ in our sisters and brothers in other lands, the El Salvadors, Panamas and Iraqs of the contemporary scene, is to begin to break the idolatry of the state, and to make visible the Body of Christ in the world. We must cease to think that the only choices open to the Church are either to withdraw into some private or 'sectarian' confinement, or to embrace the public debate policed by the state. The Church as Body of Christ transgresses both the lines which separate public from private and the borders of nation-states, thus creating spaces for a different kind of political practice, one which is incapable of being pressed into the service of wars or rumours of wars.

In the Church, then, the practices of the liturgy, the creeds, the scriptural canon, hospitality, binding and loosing, the exercise of episcopal authority, all constitute the Church as a distinctive public body.[87] Augustine goes beyond saying that the Church is public like the Roman Empire is public, however, arguing that the Empire is not public at all because its practices are not oriented toward the worship of God. A true *res publica* is based on justice, which must include giving God his due in sacrifice, for only when God is loved can there be love of others and a mutual acknowledgement of right. According to Augustine, the true public thing is thus constituted by the Eucharist, which offers true sacrifice to God and makes the Church into Christ's body.[88]

Having discussed what it means to call the Church 'public,'

---

[86] For an extended discussion of the base communities as alternative ecclesial polities, see William T. Cavanaugh, 'The Ecclesiologies of Medellín and the Lessons of the Base Communities,' *Cross Currents* vol. 44, no. 1 (Spring 1994), pp. 74–81.

[87] Hütter, 'The Church as "Public." '

[88] Augustine, XIX. §21-3, X §6.

we need also to be more precise about what it means to call the Church a 'space.' One option here is to produce a two-dimensional mapping of the nation-state, then configure the borders of the Church on this grid. Those borders could be drawn as coterminous with the borders of the nation-state (theocracy), or as an isolated island geographically within the nation-state but not participating in it (Amish), or as a space within 'civil society,' that is, within the national borders but outside the state apparatus (Murray). What these models have in common is the map, a formal figure of abstract places from which the dimension of time has been eliminated.[89] Placing the Church on such a grid is a peculiarly modern phenomenon. In medieval theology, the temporal indicated a time between the first and second comings of Christ, during which the coercive sword of civil authority, under the tutelage of the Church, was 'temporarily' necessary. One need not endorse the Constantinian arrangements of medieval Christendom to lament the fact that in modern times the temporal has become not a time but a space, a realm or sphere, one which is usually located *outside* the spiritual realm occupied by the Church.

There is a much richer concept of space to be found in the

---

[89] Michel de Certeau explains what happens when the 'trajectory' (we might substitute the word 'pilgrimage') is replaced by a mapping. The category of 'trajectory' was intended to suggest a temporal movement through space, that is the unity of a diachronic *succession* of points through which it passes, and not the *figure* that these points form on a space that is supposed to be synchronic or achronic. Indeed, this 'representation' is insufficient, precisely because a trajectory is drawn, and time and movement are thus reduced to a line that can be seized as a whole by the eye and read in a single moment, as one projects onto a map the path taken by someone walking through a city. However useful this 'flattening out' may be, it transforms the *temporal* articulation of places into a *spatial* sequence of points; Michel de Certeau, *The Practice of Everyday Life*, trans. Steven Rendall (Berkeley: University of California Press, 1984), p. 35.

work of Jesuit social theorist Michel de Certeau. Certeau contrasts the 'place' (*lieu*) of the map with 'space' (*espace*). Place is a static order in which all the elements are arranged in their proper location, *beside* one another, no two things occupying the same location. The map produces a place by means of an abstract, two-dimensional grid produced by observation, allowing surveillance and control of a particular territory. After the fifteenth century, maps gradually replaced itineraries, which had described journeys or pilgrimages in terms of the actions prescribed at different points (spend the night here, pray at this shrine, etc.). Such itineraries describe not place but space. A space takes into account the vector of time, such that different spaces are created by the ensemble of movements and actions on them. Space is produced by people performing operations on places, using things in different ways for different ends. According to Certeau it is stories that 'organize the play of changing relationships between spaces and places.'[90] For example, the stories told in history books (Manifest Destiny) and on the evening news induce belief in a national territory, which mobilizes certain actions such as participation in war. The stories told by Native Americans might, on the other hand, refract space in entirely different ways, and mobilize other types of actions. In theological terms we can think of Certeau's work here as a gloss on Augustine's conception of the two cities. They do not exist beside each other on a territorial grid, but are formed by telling different stories about ends, and by thus using matter and motion in different ways.

The Eucharistic liturgy can be understood as what Certeau calls a 'spatial story,' an operation performed on matter and place – in this case by God, with human cooperation – which produces a different kind of space. The liturgy is not a symbol

[90] Certeau, p. 118. See pp. 34–42, 115–30.

to be 'read,' its 'meaning' formally detached from its signs, internalized by the individual, and smuggled as 'attitudes' or 'values' into another space outside of the Church. Just as eating and drinking together do not merely symbolize a family, but help to constitute a family, so eating and drinking the body and blood of Christ transform the partakers into a body with a social dimension. For this reason the discipline of the Christian community has since the very beginning taken the form of excommunication; who is and who is not partaking of the table defines the spatial limit of the community gathered around the table.

David Schindler uses the home-cooked meal to illustrate how the family is a different practice of space. The home-cooked meal, Schindler says, is itself a different economy, one which *transforms* material objects and reconfigures space and time. Lest this be seen as a quaint and strictly private practice, Schindler describes how the Christian is called to extend this space into ever wider circles; the task of the Church is to 'domesticate' the world, to heal the homelessness and anomie of the modern condition by extending the 'community of persons' that exists in the family – and that mirrors the Trinitarian life – to the whole world. The Church does this by performing actions on matter and motion, space and time.[91]

To speak of the Church as a public space means, then, that Christians perform stories which transform the way space is configured. The preeminent 'spatial story' is that of the formation of the Body of Christ in the Eucharist. Imagine if Christian students, such as those involved in Public Achievement, were trained to see others not through the lens of self-

[91] David L. Schindler, 'Homelessness and the Modern Condition: The Family, Evangelization, and the Global Economy,' *Logos* 3, no. 4 (Fall 2000), pp. 34–56.

interest but as fellow members of the mystical body of Christ. Why not tell them that in taking action on the plight of undocumented workers they are not reinforcing the borders of the national territory defined by 'citizenship,' but rather building up the body of Christ, which transcends those borders, and in which all – Christian or not – have a share? This approach shares with Boyte a concern to move beyond the image of the unitary 'public square' to the fostering of a multiplicity of free spaces that are nonetheless fully public. Far from a withdrawal, this approach asserts the full public currency of the most basic Christian convictions. Furthermore, the international nature of the Church challenges the sectarian narrowness of the nation-state for whom citizenship stops at the border.

To take the Church seriously as a 'free space' would mean more than encouraging Christians to look for the public elsewhere. Boyte's work helpfully suggests that our imaginations have been limited by a narrow focus on one public forum supervised by the state. When Christians approach the creation and use of material goods, for example, we have been trained to think in terms of 'economic policy,' by which is meant the conversation in civil society and state among banks, the Federal Reserve, corporations, labour unions, Congress and other concerned parties over how the state ought to manage or not manage the flow of money, taxes, tariffs, etc. When framed in these terms, the only responsible reaction seems to be lobbying. Under certain circumstances lobbying – or, better, 'witnessing' – may be helpful. The most fruitful way to dialogue with those outside of the Church, however, is through concrete practices that do not need translation into some putatively 'neutral' language to be understood. A significant response would be creating spaces in which alternative stories about material goods are told, and alternative forms of economics are made possible. For example, churches in my area have already begun to establish relationships with CSA (community supported agriculture) farms. In CSAs, a community is formed by buying shares of a farm's produce at the beginning of the growing season, thus sharing the risks involved in farming. The community is invited to help with the work of the farm and receives the benefits of its produce. In a significant and material way, the imagination of globalization is short-circuited and replaced by an alternative economic space which gives priority to personal relationships, community responsibility, a livable income for farmers, and a direct stewardship of the land from which our food comes.

The irony implicit in the models of civil society I have examined is that in our attempts to do social justice and to make theology public, we in fact consign the Church to public irrelevance. Public theology is simply not public enough. What is lost is an important possibility of challenging in a fundamental way the dreary calculus of state and individual by creating truly free alternative spaces, cities of God in time.

THE MYTH OF GLOBALIZATION AS CATHOLICITY

There is a great deal of confusion in Christian social thought over the phenomenon known as globalization. Many who write on the Church and politics carry on as if nothing had happened, preoccupied with the question of if and how the Church should enter 'the public realm,' an imaginary national space where conflicts are settled. Globalization is left for those who deal in so-called 'economic ethics,' either to decry transnational firms paying Salvadoran textile workers 33 cents an hour, or to hail the capitalist catholicity which is including those 'currently excluded within the beneficent circle of fruitful practices,' as Michael Novak has it.[1] Those of us who have been critical of the nation-state as such are also confused. One would think that we would be pleased – or would at least find something else to do – now that the global economy has rendered national borders increasingly irrelevant. Africans and New Yorkers commune on the Internet, and the world has shrunk to proportions measurable by the click of a mouse. A catholicity undreamed by the original *Catholica* is now dawning. Ought we, like the Donatists in Augustine's phrase, sit like frogs in our swamp croaking 'We are the only Catholics,'[2] when a

---

[1] Michael Novak, *The Catholic Ethic and the Spirit of Capitalism* (New York: Free Press, 1993), p. 153.

[2] See Peter Brown, *Augustine of Hippo* (Berkeley: University of California Press, 1967), p. 221.

much broader universality is now within reach?[3] Or is it a universality at all? MacIntyre and Lyotard conversely invoke images of fragmentation to characterize the situation of late capitalism. Has the possibility of true catholicity been defeated in the triumph of global capital?

I believe that much of the Christian confusion over globalization results from a neglect of the Eucharist as the source of a truly Catholic practice of space and time. Globalization marks a certain configuration for the discipline of space and time; I would like to juxtapose this geography with another geography, a geography of the Eucharist and its production of catholicity. In the first half of this chapter, I will argue that globalization is not properly characterized by mere fragmentation, but enacts a universal mapping of space typified by detachment from any particular localities. This is not a true catholicity, however, for two reasons: first, this detachment from the particular is actually used as a discipline to reproduce divisions between rich and poor, and second, it produces fragmented subjects unable to engage a catholic imagination of space and time. Globalism is a masternarrative, the consumption of which ironically produces fragmented subjects incapable of telling a genuinely catholic story. In the second half of this chapter, I show that the Eucharist produces a catholicity which does not simply prescind from the local, but contains the universal *Catholica* within each local embodiment of the body of Christ. The body of Christ is only performed in a local Eucharistic community, and yet in the body of Christ spatial and temporal divisions are collapsed. In

---

[3] Robert H. Nelson argues that global capitalism has replaced Christianity with a far more effective means of universal salvation. For his exposition of global capitalism as theology, see *Reaching for Heaven on Earth: The Theological Meaning of Economics* (Savage, MD: Rowman and Littlefield, 1991).

the complex space of the body of Christ, attachment to the local is not a fascist nostalgia for *gemeinschaft* in the face of globalization. Consumption of the Eucharist consumes one into the narrative of the pilgrim City of God, whose reach extends beyond the global to embrace all times and places.

I. THE DOMINANCE OF THE UNIVERSAL

The 'giant sucking sound' that Ross Perot heard in 1992 was the sound of 'American' jobs being drained into Mexico as a result of NAFTA.[4] 'If he's against it, I'm for it' would be a natural reaction for someone allergic to the kind of nationalistic particularism put forth by the likes of Perot and Pat Buchanan in opposition to NAFTA. What I hope to show in this section, however, is that globalization does not signal the demise of the nation-state but is in fact a hyperextension of the nation-state's project of subsuming the local under the universal.

The rise of the modern state is marked by the triumph of the universal over the local in the sovereign state's usurpation of power from the Church, the nobility, guilds, clans, and towns.[5] The universalization of law and rights would liberate the individual from the whims of local custom, thereby creating a direct relationship, or 'simple space,' between the sovereign and the individual. As John Milbank uses the term, simple space contrasts with the complex space of overlapping loyalties and authorities in medieval society.[6] Rights did not

---

[4] The North American Free Trade Agreement, signed into law by President Clinton in 1993, eliminates all trade barriers between the US, Mexico, and Canada.

[5] Robert Nisbet details this process in his *The Quest for Community* (London: Oxford University Press, 1953), pp. 75–152.

[6] John Milbank, 'On Complex Space' in *The Word Made Strange: Theology, Language, Culture* (Oxford: Basil Blackwell, 1997), pp. 268–92.

pertain to individuals alone; local groupings were themselves possessed of rights and freedoms which were not simply conferred by a sovereign centre. These associations over-lapped in the rights and duties which individual persons owed to each other and to the different associations to which they belonged. Both the person and the local association were wholes to themselves, while each also constituting part of a larger whole. Otto Gierke's now classic work in medieval law shows how this complex conception of space was based on the Pauline theology of the body of Christ.[7]

The new configuration of space that arose with modernity is helpfully illuminated by Michel de Certeau's distinction between 'itineraries' and 'maps.' Pre-modern representations of space marked out itineraries which told 'spatial stories,' for example, the illustration of the route of a pilgrimage which gave instructions on where to pray, where to spend the night, and so on. Rather than surveying them as a whole, the pilgrim moves through particular spaces, tracing a narrative through space and time by his or her movements and practices. A fifteenth-century Aztec representation of the exodus of the Totomihuacas, for example, displays what amounts to a log of their travels: footprints accompanied by pictures of successive events from the journey, such as river crossings, meals, and battles.[8] By contrast, modernity gave rise to the mapping of space on a grid, a 'formal ensemble of abstract places' from which the itinerant was erased. A map is defined as 'a totalizing stage on which elements of diverse origin are brought together to form the tableau of a "state" of

---

[7] Otto Gierke, *Associations and Law: The Classical and Early Christian Stages*, trans. George Heiman (Toronto: University of Toronto Press, 1977), pp. 143–60.

[8] Michel de Certeau, *The Practice of Everyday Life* (Berkeley: University of California Press, 1984), p. 120.

geographical knowledge.'[9] Space itself is rationalized as homogeneous and divided into identical units. Each item on the map occupies its proper place, such that things are set beside one another, and no two things can occupy the same space. The point of view of the map user is detached and universal, allowing the entire space to be seen simultaneously.[10] The type of mapping that Certeau describes is a corollary of the rise of the modern state, which depends on the ability to survey a bounded territory from a sovereign centre and make uniform the relations of each particular unit of space to every other.

The flattening of complex social space by the modern state does not mean that local groups simply vanished with the rise of the state. Rather, local social groupings were recast as 'intermediate associations' between state and individual, and such institutions have played an important role in mediating the state project. The universal is mediated by the local; the institutions of civil society, as Hegel saw, are educative, or as Foucault would later say, disciplinary. Parties, unions, churches, families, prisons, hospitals, and schools help to embody and produce the state project. Such institutions in modernity depend on a rational mapping of space, captured well by Foucault's famous image of the Panopticon, a prison space organized around a central surveillance tower. Space is made homogeneous and uniform; each particular unit relates directly to the centre, which sees all but is not seen. Not knowing when one is being supervised, each individual becomes self-disciplining.[11]

---

[9] Certeau, p. 121.

[10] Certeau, pp. 115–30.

[11] G. W. F. Hegel, *The Philosophy of Right*, trans. T. M. Knox (Oxford: Clarendon Press, 1952), §256–7; Michel Foucault, *Discipline and Punish: The Birth of the Prison*, trans. Alan Sheridan (New York: Vintage Books, 1977), pp. 293–308.

In the political economy which precedes globalization, then, the local is subsumed under the universal, but local attachments still play an important role in mediating the universal. The Fordist economic model which reigned from World War I to the early 1970s depended on strong attachment to nation, corporation, family, community, and union. Economic historians characterize this era by reference to Henry Ford's two-fold idea of production and consumption: 1) the concentration and discipline of labour through assembly-line production in large factories, and 2) the cooperation of unions, families, and local communities in prioritizing mass consumption (the assumption being that mass production depends on the workers being able and willing to buy what they produce). The state did not simply overcome civil society, but rather the state was a diffused complex of power relations produced and reproduced in the institutions of civil society through the generation of consensus.[12]

The post-Fordist global economy currently emerging, however, goes farther than Foucault envisioned in subsuming local social groupings under the universal, to the point of detachment from any particular space. Foucault still depends on a strong account of the institutions of state and civil society. Those institutions, however, are everywhere in crisis.[13] Governments have ceded or lost control over the transnational economy; through deregulation and computer

[12] On Foucault's relationship to Hegel, see Michael Hardt, 'The Withering of Civil Society,' *Social Text* 45, vol. 14, no. 4 (Winter 1995), pp. 31–4.

[13] On the disappearance of the conditions of possibility for civil society, see Hardt, pp. 34–40; Kenneth Surin, 'Marxism(s) and "The Withering Away of the State,"' *Social Text* no. 27 (1990), pp. 42–6; and Antonio Negri, *The Politics of Subversion: A Manifesto for the Twenty-First Century* (Cambridge: Polity Press, 1989), pp. 169–99.

transfers money has become virtually stateless. The disciplinary mechanisms of the factory and the factory town are no longer necessary for the extraction of surplus labour, and have given way to part-time labour, home labour, various forms of illegal labor, and global 'outsourcing.' The subcontracting operations of multinational corporations, such as Nike in Asia, no longer demand or even allow the direct oversight or disciplining of labour by the purchasing company. Labour is hidden, and the sources of production are constantly shifting location. Unions have consequently lost much of their power. With the loss of geographical stability, family, Church, and local community have also given way to global monoculture and 'virtual community.' In sum

> 'The new order eschews loyalty to workers, products, corporate structures, businesses, factories, communities, even the nation,' the *New York Times* announces. Martin S. Davis, chair of Gulf and Western, declares, 'All such allegiances are viewed as expendable under the new rules. You cannot be emotionally bound to any particular asset.'[14]

As is often remarked, the nation-state itself is apparently giving way before the free flow of global capital. The geographical flexibility of the transnational corporation under post-Fordism produces competition between nations and localities to sacrifice their own control over wages, working conditions, and environmental standards in order to attract business. Under the conditions of the Uruguay Round of GATT, nation-states have surrendered their sovereignty over trade to the World Trade Organization, which is empowered to judge which laws enacted in any community of

---

[14] David Morris, 'Free Trade: The Great Destroyer' in Jerry Mander and Edward Goldsmith, eds., *The Case Against the Global Economy* (San Francisco: Sierra Club Books, 1996), p. 221.

the signatory nations constitute a barrier to free trade. National or local laws governing such activities as pesticide use, clear cutting of forests, and hormones in meat are subject to revocation by the WTO, from which there is no appeal.[15]

And yet the nation-state perdures as an important factor in the neutralization of opposition to globalization and its acceptance as natural and inevitable. While the Commerce Department and USAID have spent hundreds of millions to encourage US businesses to move jobs overseas,[16] the US congressional debate over NAFTA was conducted in such a way that nationalism wholly occluded the issue of class. The terms of the debate became 'Is NAFTA good or bad for America?' Absent was the possibility that the agreement eliminating the last trade barriers between North American nations might be good for *some* Americans (or Mexicans) – namely shareholders and consumers with purchasing power – and bad for *some* Americans – namely workers.

GATT and NAFTA represent a voluntary loss of sovereignty for the nation-state. This apparent act of self-sacrifice is incomprehensible unless we see that these changes do not mean the end of the state project, but rather its generalization across space. If the state project is character-ized by the subsumption of the local under the universal, then globalization hyperextends this project. Just as the nation-state freed the market from the 'interventions' of local custom,

[15] Ralph Nader and Lori Wallach, 'GATT, NAFTA, and the Subversion of the Democratic Process' in Mander and Goldsmith, eds., pp. 92–107.

[16] The article 'Losing our Shirts' in *The Independent* (Durham, NC), April 6, 1994, documents how, for example, USAID has spent over a billion dollars since 1980 on grants, loans, and advertising encouraging US companies to seek cheap labour in the Caribbean and Central America. US tax dollars have paid for USAID advertisements in trade journals, such as one that reads 'Rosa Martinez produces apparel for US markets on her sewing machine in El Salvador. *You* can hire her for 33 cents an hour.'

and freed the individual to relate to other individuals on the basis of standardized legal and monetary systems,[17] so globalization frees commerce from the nation-state, which, as it turns out, is now seen as one more localization impeding the universal flow of capital.

Advances in the management of time have made possible the extension of the universal mapping of space to a global level. The speed with which information and people can travel across space has overcome spatial barriers and shrunk the dimensions of the world. The metaphor of the 'global village' is often invoked to elicit catholic sentiments of the world's peoples coming into communion with each other, overcoming the ethnic, tribal, and traditional barriers which have produced so much bloodshed over the centuries. Global mapping appears to make all the people on earth contemporaries, sharing the same space and time. And indeed, a universal corporate culture increasingly penetrates local cultures worldwide. If one were parachuted into a shopping mall, it would take some investigation to discover whether one had touched down in Cambridge or Fort Worth, Memphis or Medicine Hat, Dar es Salaam or Minsk.

Examples of the dominance of the universal – the 'McDonaldization of Society,' to quote the title of George Ritzer's study[18] – are too common to belabour. In corporate language, the vision is often presented as a beneficent catholicity which produces peace through the overcoming of division. Utopia, says the president of Nabisco Corporation, is 'One world of homogeneous consumption ... [I am] looking forward to the day when Arabs and Americans, Latins and

[17] Anthony Giddens, *The Nation-State and Violence* (Berkeley: University of California Press, 1987), pp. 148–71.
[18] George Ritzer, *The McDonaldization of Society* (Thousand Oaks, CA: Pine Forge Press, 1993).

Scandinavians will be munching Ritz crackers as enthusias-
tically as they already drink Coke or brush their teeth with
Colgate.'[19] As I will suggest in the next section, however, the
triumph of the universal does not simply overcome spatial
barriers. Indeed, the attempt to map space as homogeneous
and catholic, overcoming spatial divisions, is often itself a ruse
to divert attention from the new forms of division that are
being produced.

II. THE DISCIPLINE OF DETACHMENT

The post-Fordist economy is marked by geographical flexibility and the overcoming of Fordist segmentation of space.
Nevertheless, all this apparent decentralization and despatia-
lization masks a different discipline of space which is in some
ways 'ever more tightly organized *through* dispersal.'[20] Workers
in one location will be much more compliant to the demands of
management if the company has the capability to close the
plant and move operations somewhere else where wages and
other standards are lower. The domination of space becomes
detached from any particular localities and becomes a matter
of the abstract and universal potentiality of *any* space to
produce profit. Domination of space relies less on direct
supervision and more on information, an accurate and up-to-
the-minute mapping of labour markets and exchange rates
worldwide which gives the corporation mobility.[21] Now the
panopticon does not simply characterize the discipline of space
within a particular location, such as a factory. It characterizes
the gaze spread over the entire map of the globe.

[19] Quoted in Jerry Mander, 'The Rules of Corporate Behavior,' in
Mander and Goldsmith, eds., p. 321.
[20] David Harvey, *The Condition of Postmodernity* (Oxford: Basil Blackwell,
1989), p. 159.
[21] Harvey, pp. 159–60, 233–9.

Gilles Deleuze's concept of the 'line of flight' is often invoked as an image of resistance to highly segmented and disciplined spaces. One creates 'nomad spaces' of flight from territorialization, the surveillance and control of space. The irony here is that in the globalized economy direct discipline over a particular locality has given way to the discipline of sheer mobility, the ability to flee. The transnational corporation's flight to another location on the map is based on the mapping itself, and only serves to increase control over the workers. Deleuze and Guattari do acknowledge the inevitable reterritorialization of flight; they ask rhetorically 'Do not even lines of flight, due to their eventual divergence, reproduce the very formations their function it was to dismantle and outflank?'[22] In the post-Fordist economy, however, reproduction of these formations is not a divergence; the whole *point* of flight is to reproduce these formations. Globalization has complicated any dichotomy between the oppressive mapping of a fixed space, and a nomadic resistance to that mapping. In globalization, flight is facilitated by the universal mapping itself, and flight reproduces the segmentation of space.

Far from yielding peaceful flight, the compression of space in the 'global village' has not only exacerbated but produced insecurity and conflict in the late twentieth century, since global mapping brings diverse localities into competition with

---

[22] Gilles Deleuze and Félix Guattari, *A Thousand Plateaus*, trans. Brian Massumi (Minneapolis: University of Minnesota Press, 1987), p. 13. There is a difficulty in terminology here because Deleuze and Guattari use the term 'map' in almost the exact opposite way that Certeau uses it. For Deleuze and Guattari, a 'tracing' is a 'competence' which homogenizes and captures space. A 'map,' on the other hand, is 'rhizomatic' and productive of lines of flight; Deleuze and Guattari, pp. 12–20.

one another.[23] Globalization increases potentially deadly competition among nation-states, since free trade is paradoxically put forth as a competitive development strategy for particular countries. Through transcending spatial barriers, capital is able to map and exploit even minute spatial differentiations, unleashing an economic war of all against all.[24]

Competition produces an apparent attachment to the local, for in an effort to lure capital, diverse places must emphasize what is unique and advantageous to their location (cheap wages, weak unions, good resources and infrastructure, lax regulation, attractive environment for management, etc.). Yet at the same time, competition paradoxically increases detachment from the local, for as localities compete for capital, the supposed uniqueness of each local place is increasingly tailored to attract development, modelled on those localities that have previously been successful. David Harvey puts the paradox in these terms: 'the less important the spatial barriers, the greater the sensitivity of capital to the variations of place within space, and the greater the incentive for places to be differentiated in ways attractive to capital.'[25]

An ephemeral particularity is therefore merely the flipside of a dominant universality. Mexican food is popularized in places like Minnesota, but its dominant form is the fast-food chain Taco Bell, which serves up a hot sauce that a native Minnesotan could mistake for ketchup. Nevertheless, just as

[23] See, for example, Helena Norberg-Hodge, 'The Pressure to Modernize and Globalize' in Mander and Goldsmith, eds., pp. 33–46. Norberg-Hodge traces the destructive influence of globalization on the traditional culture of the Ladakhi people of northern India. She argues that ethnic conflicts in India are produced largely by the competition, artificial scarcity, and unrealizable desires created by globalization.

[24] Harvey, pp. 271, 293–6.

[25] Harvey, pp. 295–6.

the food must be universalized and made bland enough to appeal potentially to the taste of *anyone anywhere*, to compete there must be a simultaneous emphasis on its unique qualities; advertised images must be rooted in a particular location, for example, the traditional Mexican culture of the *abuelita* before the clay oven, sipping *pulque* and shaping tortillas in the palm of her hand. Anyone who has stood at a Taco Bell counter and watched a surly white teenager inject burritos with a sour cream gun knows how absurd these images are, not just because Taco Bell does not conform to the Mexican reality, but because the *abuelita* herself is a manufactured image. Today's Mexican woman is more likely to wash down her tortillas with a can of Diet Coke, while sitting before dubbed reruns of 'Dynasty.' The more 'muy auténtico' a place claims to be, the more it exposes itself as a simulacrum, a copy of a copy for which there exists no original.[26]

Global mapping produces the illusion of diversity by the juxtaposition of all the varied products of the world's traditions and cultures in one space and time in the marketplace. Mexican food and tuna hotdish, mangoes and mayonnaise all meet the gaze of the consumer. For the consumer with money, the illusion is created that all the world's peoples are contemporaries occupying the same space-time. It is important that the other be 'different,' but it is equally important, as Ken Surin puts it, that the other be '*merely* different.'[27] The production of the simulacrum,

---

[26] I have in my possession an illustration of a young man, arms spread wide, standing on a beautiful desert highway. Superimposed around him are the slogans, 'discover difference,' 'seek the unusual,' 'take another road,' 'forget typical,' 'nothing ordinary about it,' 'leave ordinary behind.' The illustration is printed on a paper tray liner from Taco Bell.

[27] Kenneth Surin, 'A Certain "Politics of Speech": "Religious Pluralism" in the Age of the McDonald's Hamburger,' *Modern Theology* 7/1 (October 1990), p. 74.

difference at the surface only, precludes engagement with the genuinely other. So the conceit is advanced that my consumption contributes to your well-being through mutually beneficial global trade; my eating slakes your hunger.[28] The consumption of others' particularity absorbs them into a simulated catholicity while it simultaneously hides the way that space remains rigidly segmented between the Minnesotans who enjoy mangoes in the dead of winter and the Brazilian Indians who earn forty cents an hour picking them.

While globalization markets the traditions of the local culture, the people who inhabit the latter space are often losing their own traditions to the universal culture of Coke and Colgate. Historical continuity is difficult to maintain in the whirlwind of flexible accumulation. Local attachments are loosed by the centrifuge of ephemeral desire, which is fuelled by global capitalism's ever accelerating need for growth. The post-Fordist economy has pursued ever-increasing rates of turnover, most significantly by developing markets addicted to quickly changing fashion, and by shifting emphasis from goods to services, which have a much shorter 'shelf-life.' Short-term planning is endemic. Disposability, not simply of goods, but of relationships and particular attachments of any kind, is the hallmark of consumption in the new economy.[29] The result is not merely the dominance of a few name brands; the search for demand mandates a proliferation of specialized and exotic products (for example, bottled water for dogs or gourmet coffee beans recovered from Sumatran luwak

[28] The latter phrase is taken from Catherine Pickstock's brilliant exposition of the logic of the Eucharist in medieval Europe in her *After Writing: On the Liturgical Consummation of Philosophy* (Oxford: Basil Blackwell, 1998), pp. 121–66. Pickstock adopts the phrase from a Reformation controversy over the Eucharist.

[29] Harvey, pp. 284–6.

dung[30]). The local and particular are prized precisely because of their novelty. The ideal consumer, however, is detached from all particulars. Novelty wears off, and particulars become interchangeable; what is desired is desire itself. The global economy is characterized by the production of desire as its own object, or as Fredric Jameson says, 'the consumption of sheer commodification as a process.'[31]

In this economy images themselves have become commodities, and are prized as commodities precisely because of their ephemerality. Images are not only subject to a very rapid turnover, but they also easily transcend spatial barriers in a way that goods cannot. The depthlessness of these images obeys the logic of the simulacrum. The logic of exchange value has almost entirely extinguished the memory of use value.[32]

As a result, the subject is radically decentred, cast adrift in a sea of disjointed and unrelated images. If identity is forged by unifying the past, present, and future into a coherent narrative sequence, the ephemerality and rapid change of images deconstructs this ability. The late capitalist subject becomes 'schizophrenic,' in Lacan's terms, and experiences only 'a series of pure and unrelated presents in time.'[33] But this new construction or deconstruction of subjectivity is inaccurately described as pure heterogeneity, the triumph of the particular. For the subject created is the Nabisco executive's universal homogeneous consumer, whose 'catholic' tastes preclude him from attachment to any particular narratives. Yet this by no means signals simply 'the end of masternarratives,' as Lyotard would have it. It is instead a

---

[30] Unfortunately, I'm not making these up.

[31] Fredric Jameson, *Postmodernism, or, the Cultural Logic of Late Capitalism* (Durham, NC: Duke University Press, 1991), p. x.

[32] Jameson, p. 18.

[33] Jameson, p. 27.

new catholicity, or, to quote Jameson, 'the return of narrative as the narrative of the end of narratives.'[34]

III. THE WORLD IN A WAFER

Does the Eucharist offer a counter-narrative of global proportions? Surely the Eucharist is to be done so that *from east to west* a perfect offering might be made to the glory of his name. Aquinas defines the catholicity of the Church in the broadest possible terms, as transcending all boundaries of space and time, as well as natural and social divisions among people.

> The Church is Catholic, i.e. universal, first with respect to place, because it is everywhere in the world, against the Donatists ... This Church, moreover, has three parts. One is on earth, another is in heaven, and the third is in purgatory. Secondly, the Church is universal with respect to the state of humanity, because no one is rejected, whether master or slave, male or female ... Thirdly, it is universal with respect to time ... because this Church began from the time of Abel and will last to the end of the world.[35]

The true catholicity produced by the Eucharist, however, does not depend on the mapping of global space. The Church gathered in the catacombs, after all, was as catholic as the Church that would ride Constantine's chariots to the ends of the known world.[36] I will argue in the second half of this

---

[34] Jameson, p. xii.

[35] Thomas Aquinas, *Oposculum VII*, 'In Symbolum Apostulorum, scil., Credo in Deum, Expositio,' quoted in Avery Dulles, *The Catholicity of the Church* (Oxford: Clarendon Press, 1985), p. 181.

[36] See Oliver O'Donovan's comments on the charge of 'sectarianism' in *The Desire of the Nations: Rediscovering the Roots of Political Theology* (Cambridge: Cambridge University Press, 1996), p. 216.

chapter that the Eucharist overcomes the dichotomy of universal and local. The action of the Eucharist collapses spatial divisions not by sheer mobility but by gathering in the local assembly. The *Catholica* is not a place, however, but a 'spatial story' about the origin and destiny of the whole world, a story enacted in the Eucharist.

The Greek adjective *katholikos* – derived from *kath' holou*, 'on the whole' – in antiquity was commonly used as an equivalent of 'universal' or 'general.' The earliest patristic application of the term to the Church, however, is not univocal; by 'catholic' some imply 'universal' or 'total,' but others imply 'authentic.' By the middle of the fourth century, the term has taken on more precise meaning as that which distinguishes the great Church as a whole from dissident or heretical Christian groups.[37] Although we continue to use the word 'catholic' in English as an equivalent of universal, as Henri de Lubac points out, the terms in some senses diverge. 'Universal' suggests spreading out; 'catholic' suggests gathering together. In modern English 'universal' indicates a reality prevalent everywhere. According to de Lubac ' "Catholic" says something more and different: it suggests the idea of an organic whole, of a cohesion, of a firm synthesis, of a reality which is not scattered but, on the contrary, turned toward a center which assures its unity, whatever the expanse in area or the internal differentiation might be.'[38]

The centre toward which the true *Catholica* is turned is the Eucharist which, in de Lubac's famous phrase, makes the Church. However, the Eucharist is a decentred centre; it is celebrated in the multitude of local churches scattered

---

[37] Dulles, *The Catholicity of the Church* (Oxford: Clarendon Press, 1985) p. 14.
[38] Henri de Lubac, *The Motherhood of the Church*, trans. Sr Sergia Englund (San Francisco: Ignatius Press, 1982), p. 174.

throughout the world, with a great diversity of rites, music, and liturgical spaces. It is precisely this fact that complexifies the calculus of particular and universal within the Church catholic. As Hans Urs von Balthasar puts it, 'The *Catholica* is in fact a region whose middle point is everywhere (where the Eucharist is celebrated); and (structurally) she can theoretically be everywhere: geographically, her periphery extends to "the very ends of the earth" (Rev. 1.8), a periphery that in any case can never be far from the midpoint.'[39] As Balthasar goes on to say, however, the normal condition of the *Catholica* is not Christendom – a permanent place with borders defensible by force – but diaspora. Although the Church is catholic in its missionary imperative to spread the gospel to the ends of the earth, catholicity is not dependent on extension through space.

The Eucharist celebrated in the scattered local communities is, nevertheless, gathered up into one. From the early Church, this principle was expressed by the participation of at least two bishops, as heads of local eucharistic communities, in the ordination of another bishop.[40] In the ancient Roman liturgy, at the papal Mass, a particle of the host was set aside for the following Mass. Other particles were sent out to priests celebrating Mass in the various localities.[41] In such practices the Body of Christ is not partitioned, for the whole Body of Christ is present in each fraction of the elements: the world in a wafer.

By the same liturgical action, not *part* but the *whole* Body of Christ is present in each local Eucharistic assembly. In

[39] Hans Urs von Balthasar, *Explorations in Theology IV: Spirit and Institution*, trans. Edward Oakes, SJ (San Francisco: Ignatius Press, 1995), pp. 65–6.

[40] John Zizioulas, *Being as Communion: Studies in Personhood and the Church* (Crestwood, NY: St Vladimir's Seminary Press, 1985), p. 155.

[41] de Lubac, p. 206.

Romans 16.23 Paul refers to the local community as *hole he ekklesia*, the whole Church. Indeed, in the first three centuries the term 'catholic Church' is most commonly used to identify the local church gathered around the Eucharist.[42] Each particular church is not an administrative division of a larger whole, but is in itself a 'concentration' of the whole. The whole Catholic Church is qualitatively present in the local assembly, because the whole Body of Christ is present there.[43] Catholic space, therefore, is not a simple, universal space uniting individuals directly to a whole; the Eucharist refracts space in such a way that one becomes more united to the whole the more tied one becomes to the local. The true global village is not simply a village writ large, but rather 'where two or three are gathered in my name' (Matt. 18.20).

The transcendence of spatial and temporal barriers does not depend on a global mapping, therefore, but rather on a collapsing of the world into the local assembly. It is crucial to note that, for the early Church, the eucharistic assembly would be the only one in a particular city. The Eucharist would therefore unite all the members of the Church in a particular location, regardless of age, race, sex, language, or social class. As John Zizioulas notes, gathering in solidarity and love was not a Christian innovation. Members of Roman *collegia* addressed each other as brethren and often held goods in common. What distinguished the Christian eucharistic community was the way that it transcended natural and

---

[42] de Lubac comments in a footnote that, while Zizioulas' claim that during the first three centuries the term 'catholic Church' was used *only* for the local church is a bit exaggerated, 'it was nevertheless enough for the difference from "universal" to become apparent'; de Lubac, p. 177 n. 23.

[43] de Lubac, pp. 199–202. de Lubac uses 'local church' to designate bodies such as the Eastern Rite Churches which possess their own liturgical usage and disciplines. For the purposes of this essay, I use 'local' and 'particular' interchangeably to refer to the community gathered around the Eucharist in a particular place.

social divisions. In Christ there is no Jew or Greek, slave or free, male or female (Gal. 3.28).[44] This remarkable collapsing of spatial barriers is what makes the local community truly catholic.

IV. THE EUCHARIST AS SPATIAL STORY

I have tried to show how the Eucharist breaks down the dichotomy of universal and local, but the suspicion may arise that Eucharist as antidote to globalism is simply a retreat into a place-bound theocracy or sect. Certainly the Eucharist – as in some medieval Corpus Christi rites – can be used to reinforce a fixed social hierarchy within a certain location, and to exclude others, especially the Jews, from that space.[45] Aren't all Christian attempts to privilege the local similarly subject to the fascist temptation, or the temptation of 'sectarianism,' the very antithesis of a catholicity which seeks to unify rather than divide?

In this final section of this chapter, I will argue that the *Catholica* enacted by the Eucharist is not a place as such, but a story which performs certain spatial operations on places. I will draw once again on Certeau's discussion of spatial stories, and his useful distinction between maps and itineraries. Stories organize and link spaces in a narrative sequence. They not only move from one space to another, but more accurately construct spaces through the practices of characters who trace an itinerary through the story. In contrast to the global and abstract mapping of space, medieval representations of space measured distance in hours or days, the time it would take to

---

[44] Zizioulas, pp. 150–2.

[45] See Miri Rubin, *Corpus Christi: The Eucharist in Late Medieval Culture* (Cambridge: Cambridge University Press, 1991), and Sarah Beckwith, *Christ's Body: Identity, Culture, and Society in Late Medieval Writings* (London: Routledge, 1993).

arrive at a destination on foot. These itineraries told stories about the way that was made by the pilgrims themselves as they walked toward their destinations.[46]

The itinerary implies not seeing but going; the subject does not survey the space detached as from above but is immersed in the movements indicated by the story. A story is not simply told but performed; space is organized by a body in movement, its gestures and practices. As such, the spatial story is not simply descriptive, but prescriptive. Stories give us a way to walk; 'They make the journey, before or during the time the feet perform it.'[47] As Certeau says, the story 'opens a legitimate *theater* for practical *actions*.'[48]

The spatial story is an act of resistance to the dominant overcoding of the map. And yet it does not depend on establishing its own place, its own territory to defend. Instead it moves on pilgrimage through the places defined by the map and transforms them into alternative spaces through its practices. The City of God makes use of this world as it moves through it on pilgrimage to its heavenly home. But this pilgrimage is not the detachment from any and all spaces, the sheer mobility of globalism. The Eucharist journeys by telling a story of cosmic proportions within the particular face-to-face encounter of neighbours and strangers in the local eucharistic gathering. In an economy of hypermobility, we resist not by fleeing, but by abiding.[49] The community may journey without leaving its particular location, because the

---

[46] Certeau, pp. 115–30.

[47] Certeau, p. 116.

[48] Certeau, p. 125.

[49] Frederick Bauerschmidt suggests that Certeau did not fully appreciate the way that resistance to certain practices often necessitates institutions such as monasteries and soup kitchens which, although appearing quite stationary, are a way of walking; see 'Walking in the Pilgrim City,' *New Blackfriars* 77, no. 909 (November 1996), pp. 504–17.

entire world and more comes to it in the Eucharist. The Letter to the Hebrews informs the humble community that they are not alone at their Eucharist.

> You have come to Mount Zion and to the city of the living God, the heavenly Jerusalem, and to innumerable angels in festal gathering, and to the assembly of the firstborn who are enrolled in heaven, and to God the judge of all, and to the spirits of the righteous made perfect, and to Jesus, the mediator of a new covenant, and to the sprinkled blood that speaks a better word than the blood of Abel (Heb. 12.22–4).

Though the eschatological dimension of the Eucharist is only recently being reemphasized, the patristic writings and ancient liturgies are replete with the vivid transgression of spatial and temporal barriers at the Eucharist to unite the whole Church on earth with the Church of all times and places in eternity.[50] The Eucharist not only tells but *performs* a narrative of cosmic proportions, from the death and resurrection of Christ, to the new covenant formed in his blood, to the future destiny of all creation. The consumer of the Eucharist is no longer the schizophrenic subject of global capitalism, awash in a sea of unrelated presents, but walks into a story with a past, present, and future.

In the detached hypermobility of global capitalism, signs and locations become interchangeable, for what is desired is desire itself. Augustine's lament 'I was in love with love'[51] captures this condition. Augustine saw that one's true identity is only found in desire for God, who is beyond the fleeting things of this world. We might add that it is precisely God's

---

[50] See Geoffrey Wainwright, *Eucharist and Eschatology* (New York: Oxford University Press, 1981).

[51] Augustine, *Confessions* III, 1, trans. Henry Chadwick (Oxford: Oxford University Press, 1991), p. 35.

transcendence of the world that allows liturgical difference, for where God cannot be fully grasped, a diversity of locations and practices is necessary to imply the transcendent.[52] Nevertheless, liturgical difference is possible not because all particular signs are interchangeable. On the contrary, in the Eucharist the particular is of the utmost importance, for this particular piece of bread at this particular place and time *is* the body of Christ, and is not merely a pointer to some abstract transcendent standing behind the sign. In the Eucharist there is a hypostatic union between reality and sign, *res et sacramentum*. Christ saturates the sign, such that consumption of the Eucharist identifies the consumer with God.[53]

In the Eucharist, the consumer does not stand detached from the consumed. Through consuming the eucharistic bread we are in fact consumed by the body of Christ. Augustine reports Christ's words to him: 'I am the food of the fully grown; grow and you will feed on me. And you will not change me into you like the food your flesh eats, but you will be changed into me.'[54] It should be clear that calling the Eucharist a 'story' by no means denies the reality of transubstantiation. It is the very body and blood of Christ that organize the spaces into which we walk. It is Christ, not we, who tells the story. Each consumer of the Eucharist receives the whole body of Christ, though the body remains one throughout the whole world. This is only possible because

[52] Catherine Pickstock makes this point in her 'Liturgy, Art and Politics,' forthcoming in *Modern Theology*.

[53] Jean-Luc Marion, *God without Being*, trans. Thomas A. Carlson (Chicago: University of Chicago Press, 1991), p. 156; also Frederick Bauerschmidt, 'Aesthetics: The Theological Sublime' in *Radical Orthodoxy: A New Theology*, eds. John Milbank, Catherine Pickstock, Graham Ward (London: Routledge, 1999).

[54] Augustine, VII, 10, p. 124.

the consumer is absorbed into the body. The consumer of the Eucharist begins to walk in the strange landscape of the body of Christ, while still inhabiting a particular earthly place. Now the worldly landscape is transformed by the intrusions of the universal body of Christ in the particular interstices of local space. Turn the corner, and the cosmic Christ appears in the homeless person asking for a cup of coffee. Space is constantly 'interrupted' by Christ himself, who appears in the person of the weakest, those who are hungry or thirsty, strangers or naked, sick or imprisoned (Matt. 25.31–46).

Practising the narrative of the body of Christ collapses spatial barriers, but in a way very different from globalizing capitalism. Globalization depends on a mapping that juxtaposes people from all over the world in the same space-time. This juxtaposition situates diverse localities in competition with one another. At the same time, the illusion is fostered that the world's people are contemporaries, different from each other, but *merely* different. In Eucharistic space, by contrast, we are not juxtaposed but identified. In the body of Christ, as Paul says, 'If one member suffers, all suffer together with it; if one member is honoured, all rejoice together with it' (1 Cor. 12.26).[55] This radical collapsing of spatial barriers accomplishes not competition, but says Paul, greater honour and care for the weakest member, who is identified with oneself. At the same time the other is not merely different but wholly other, for the suffering are

---

[55] Jerome Murphy-O'Connor stresses that Paul had in mind much more than 'fellowship,' but a real 'co-existence' in the body of Christ, that is, a common source of life. The community is one, and the community is Christ; 'Eucharist and Community in First Corinthians' in *Living Bread, Saving Cup: Readings on the Eucharist*, ed. R. Kevin Seasoltz (Collegeville, MN: The Liturgical Press, 1982), pp. 1–30.

identified with Christ himself (Col. 1.24), who nevertheless remains other to the Church.

In its organization of space, therefore, the Eucharist does not simply tell the story of a united human race, but brings to light barriers where they actually exist. When Paul discovers that the Corinthians are unworthily partaking of the Lord's supper because of the humiliation of the poor by the rich, Paul tells them 'Indeed, there have to be factions among you, for only so will it become clear who among you are genuine' (1 Cor. 11.19). This verse is puzzling unless we consider that the Eucharist can be falsely told as that which unites Christians around the globe while in fact some live off the hunger of others. Theologians of the southern hemisphere remind us that the imperative of 'Church unity' is often a cover for exploitation of the worst kind. In the North American context, many of our Eucharistic celebrations too have been colonized by a banal consumerism and global sentimentality. The logic of globalization infects the liturgical life of the Church itself; Christ is betrayed again at every Eucharist. Where the body is not properly discerned, Paul reminds the Corinthians, consumption of the Eucharist can make you sick or kill you (1 Cor. 11.30). This might explain the condition of some of our churches.

I will close with an illustration of how the Eucharist can operate as a spatial discipline which suggests resistance to the pretence of one united world advanced by globalizing capital. On February 13, 1977, Fr Rutilio Grande of El Salvador gave a homily during Mass in the village of Apopa.

> The Lord God gave us ... a material world for all, without borders ... 'I'll buy half of El Salvador. Look at all my money. That'll give me the right to it.' ... No! That's denying God! There *is* no 'right' against the masses of the people! A material world for all, then, without borders, without frontiers. A common table,

with broad linens, a table for everybody, like this Eucharist. A chair for everybody. And a table setting for everybody. Christ had good reason to talk about his kingdom as a meal. He talked about meals a lot. And he celebrated one the night before his supreme sacrifice ... And he said that this was the great memorial of the redemption: a table shared in brotherhood, where all have their position and place ... This is the love of a communion of sisters and brothers that smashes and casts to the earth every sort of barrier and prejudice and that one day will overcome hatred itself.[56]

Less than a month later, Rutilio Grande was gunned down by a government-sponsored death squad. In response, Archbishop Oscar Romero took the extraordinary measure of declaring that only one Mass, the funeral Mass, would be celebrated in the Archdiocese that Sunday. All the faithful, rich and poor, would be forced into a single space around the celebration of the Eucharist. The elite reacted with outrage, but Romero stood firm.[57] He was drawing on the power of the Eucharist to collapse the spatial barriers separating the rich and the poor, not by surveying the expanse of the Church and declaring it universal and united, but by gathering the faithful in one particular location around the altar, and realizing the heavenly universal *Catholica* in one place, at one moment, on earth.

[56] Rutilio Grande, SJ, quoted in Jon Sobrino, *Jesus in Latin America* (Maryknoll, NY: Orbis Books, 1987), pp. 96–7.

[57] An account of the debate over the single Mass can be found in James R. Brockman, *Romero: A Life* (Maryknoll, NY: Orbis Books, 1989), pp. 9–18.

INDEX

123